AF255159

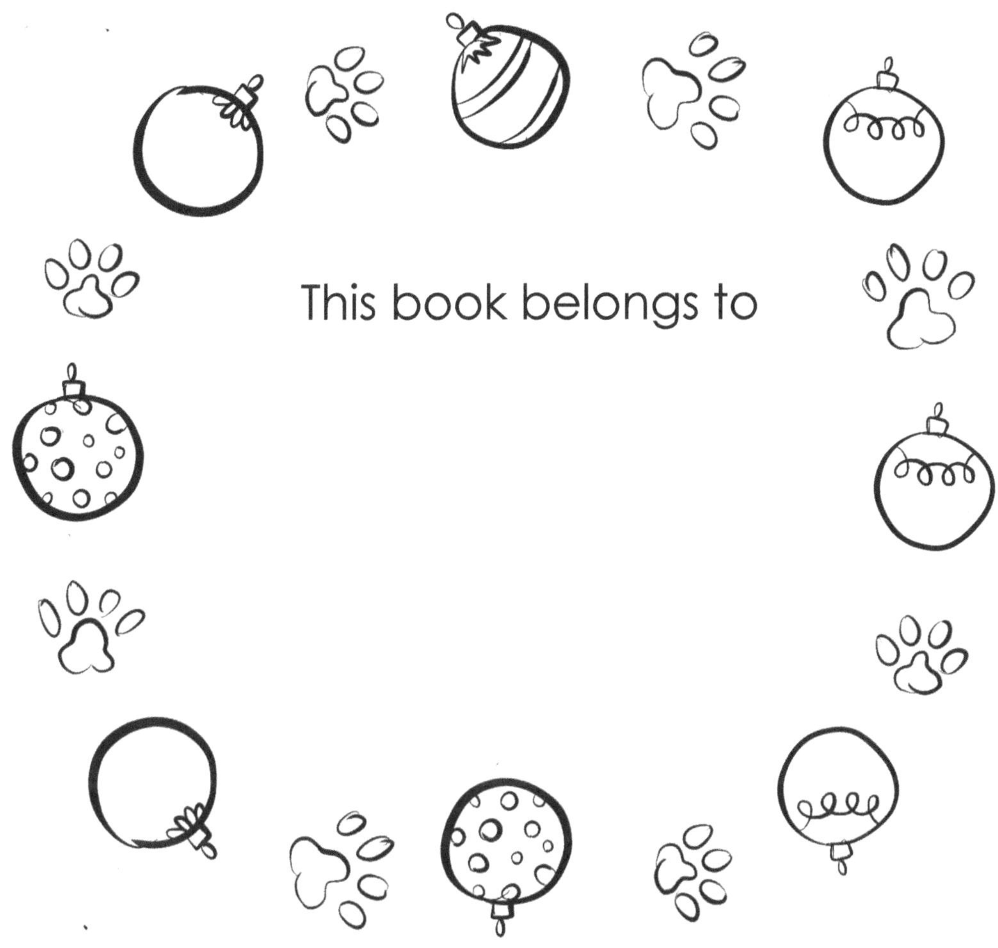

Published in 2017 by Pink Coffee Publishing, Australia.

© Amy Curran (www.amycurranillustrator.com)

All Rights Reserved. No part of this publication may be reproduced or transmitted in any form or by any means, electronic or mechanical, including photocopy, recording, or any information storage and retrieval system, without permission in writing from Amy Curran.

ISBN: 978-0-9945595-6-2

Printed in Australia.

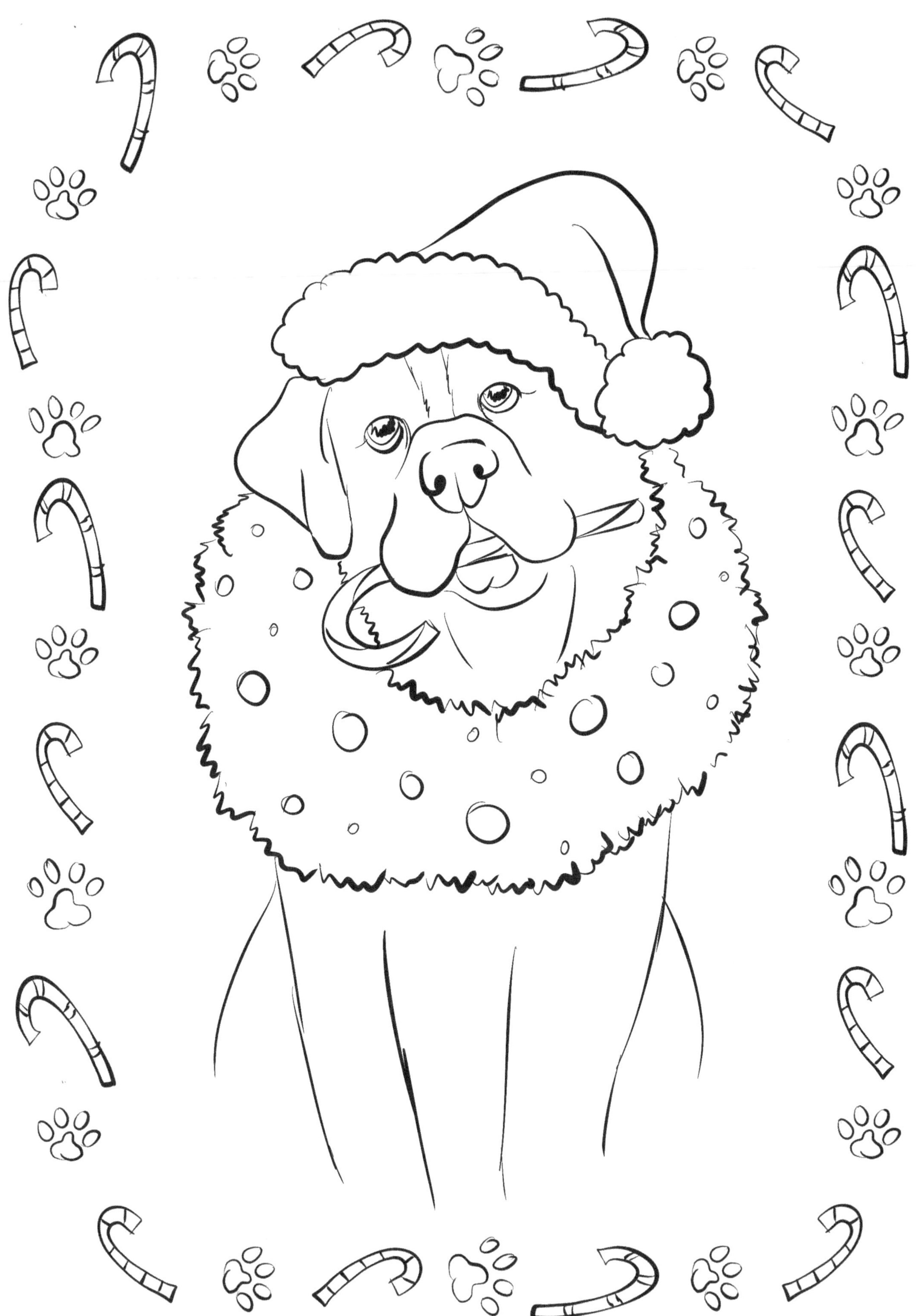

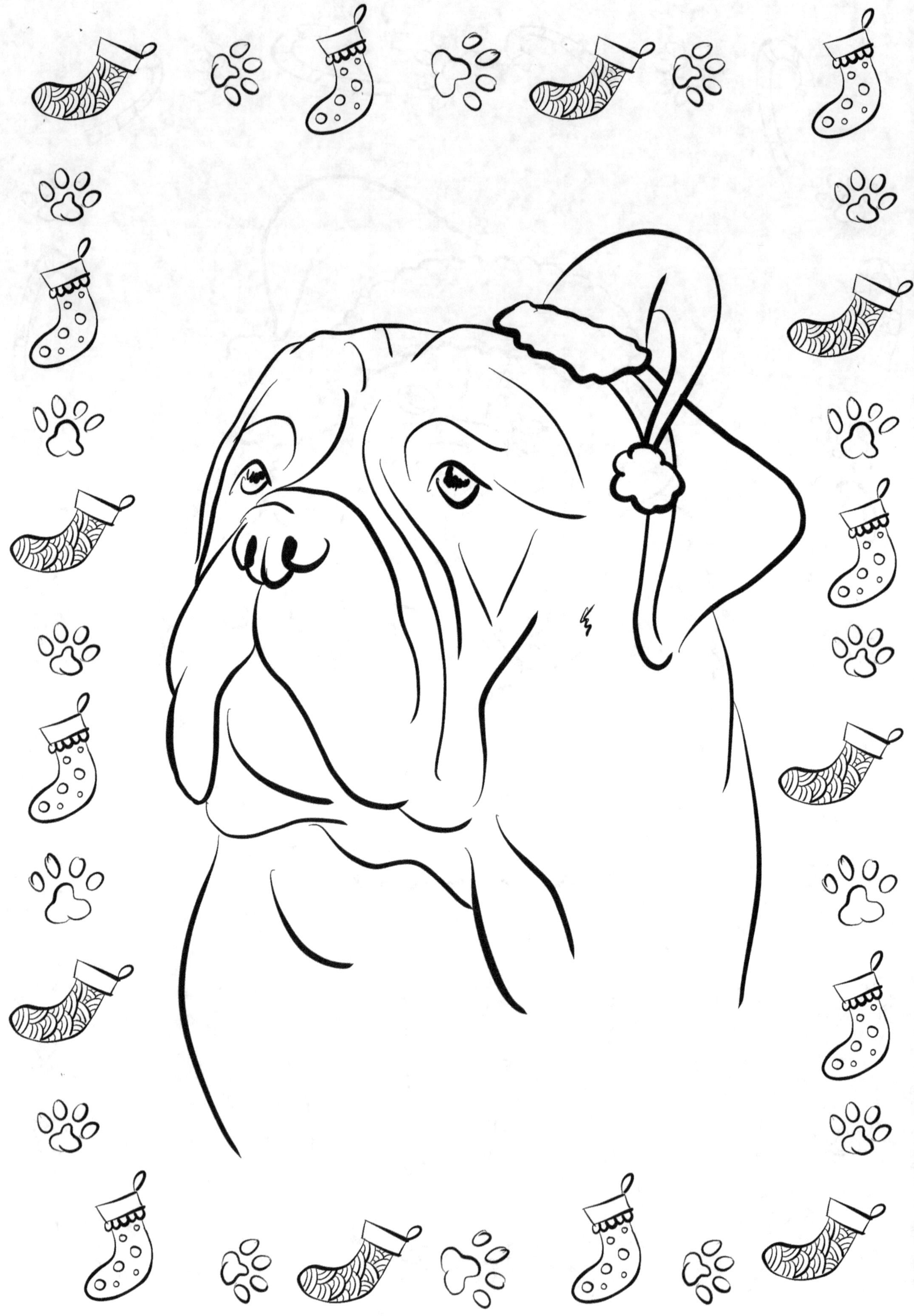

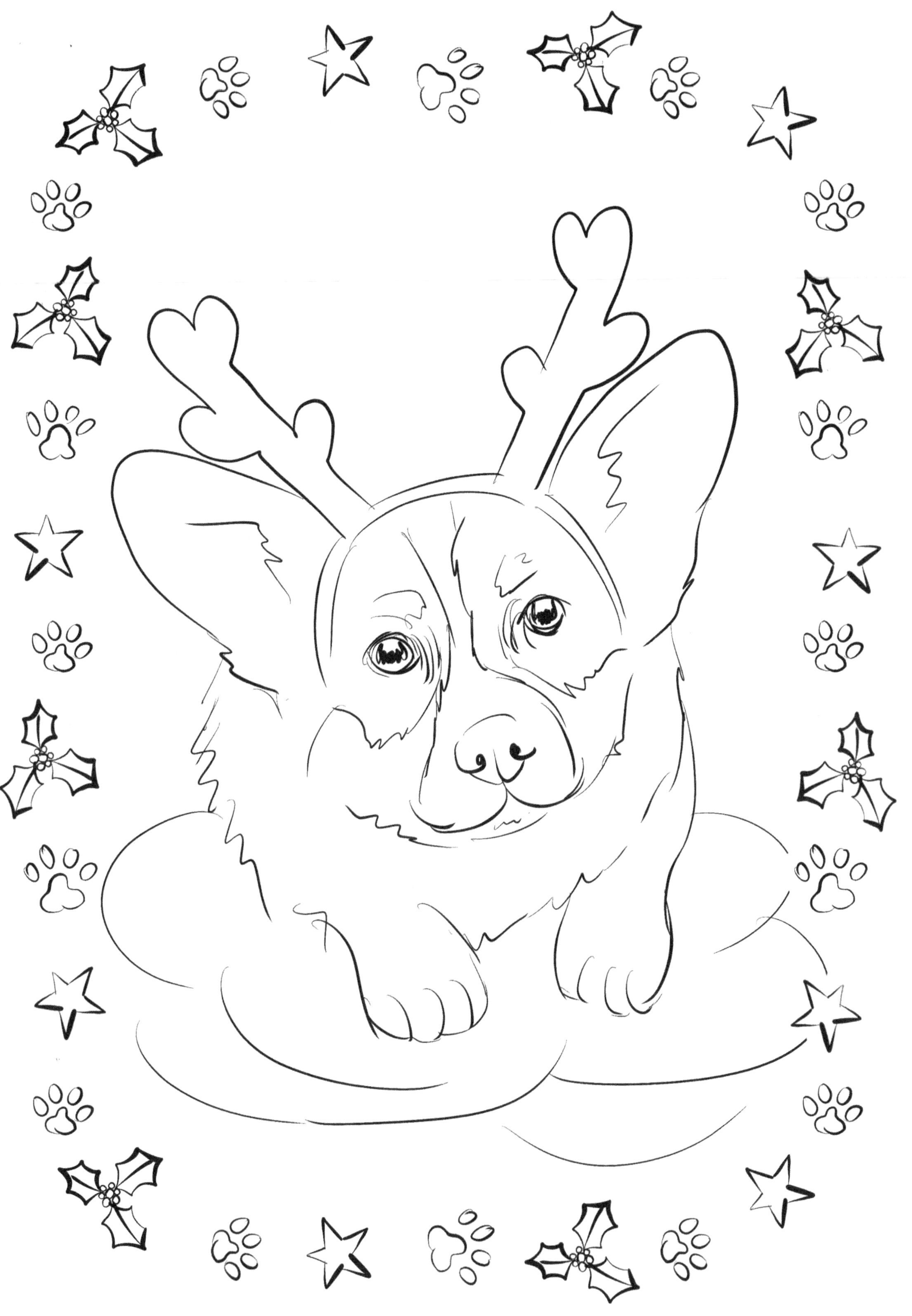

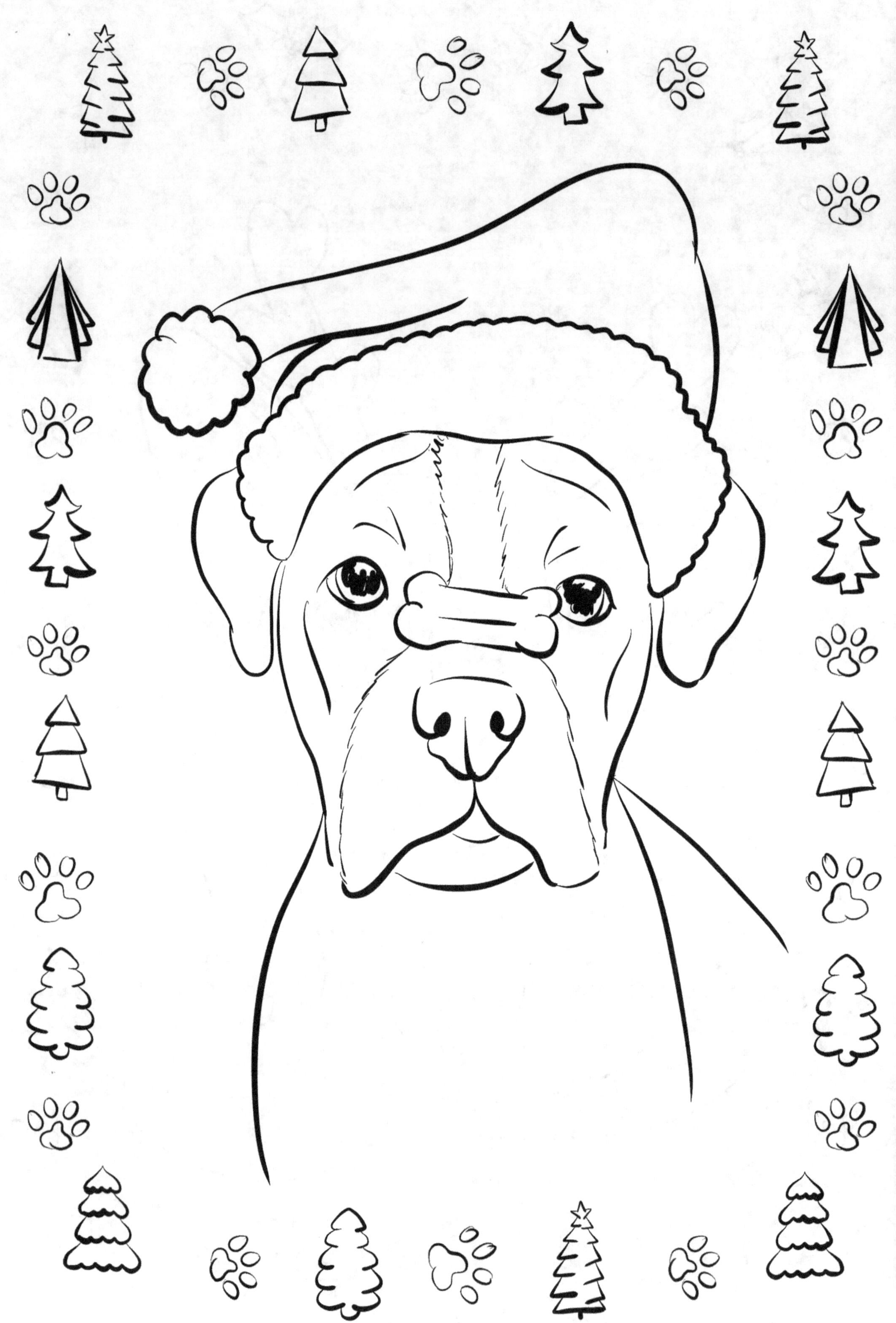

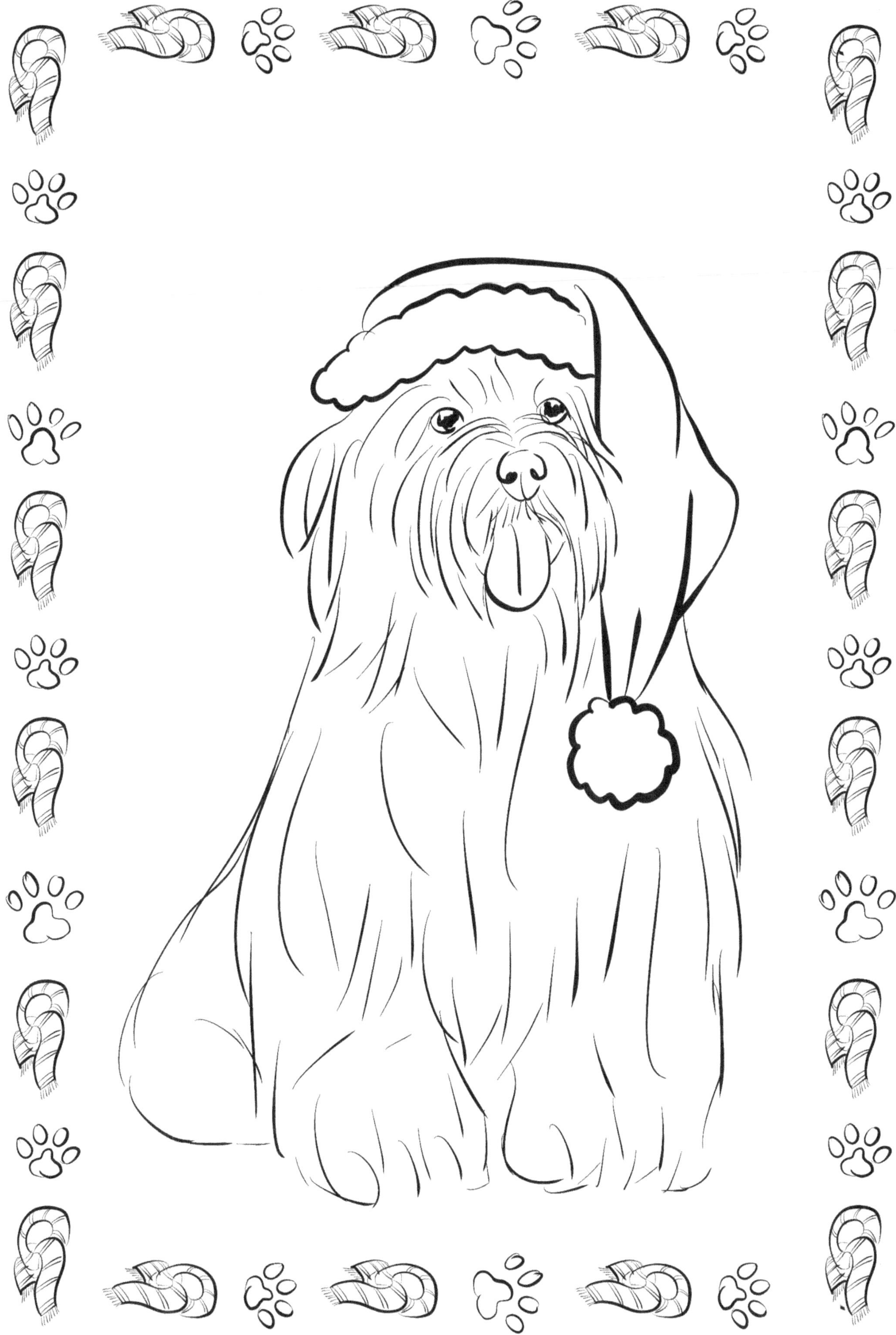

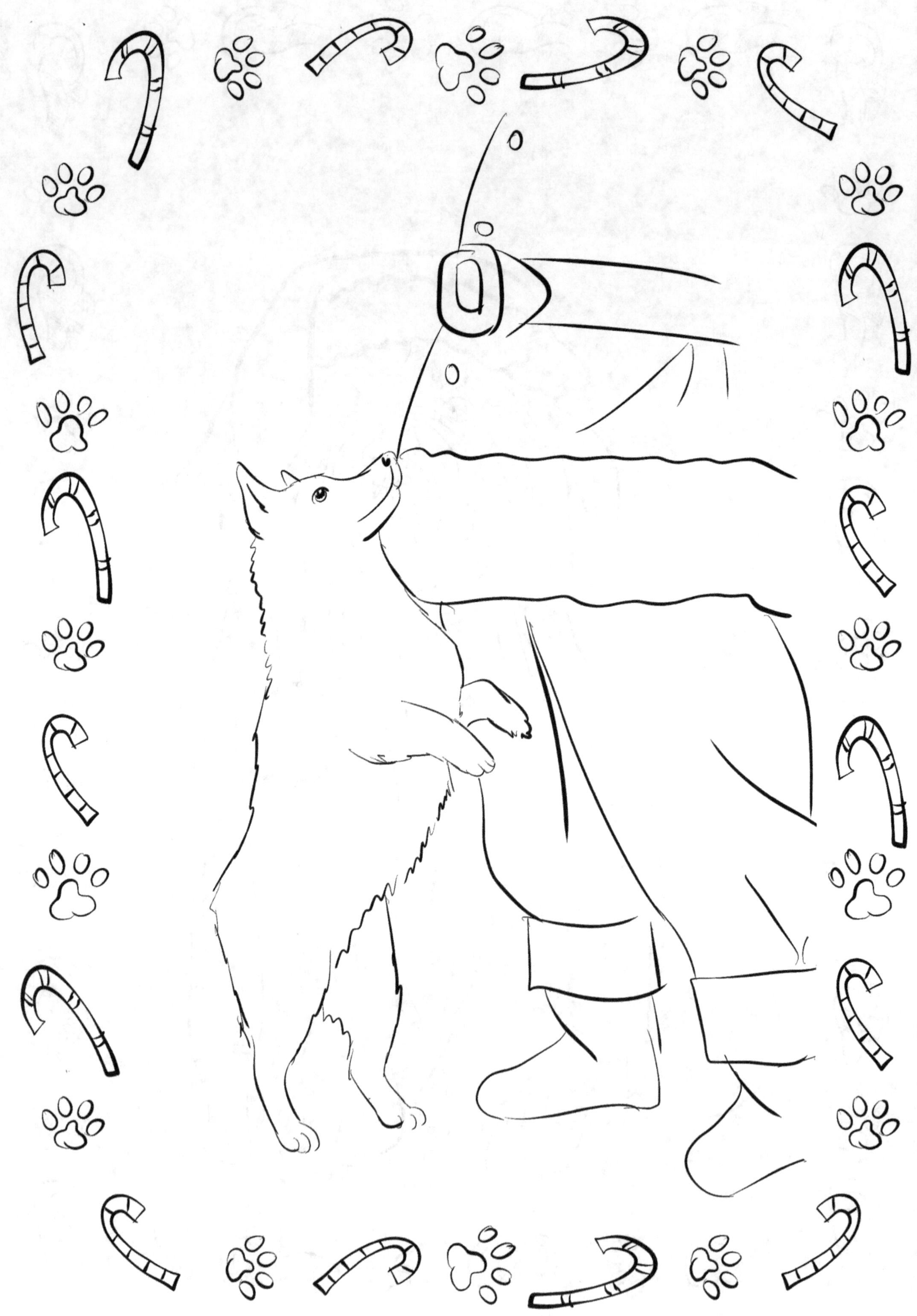

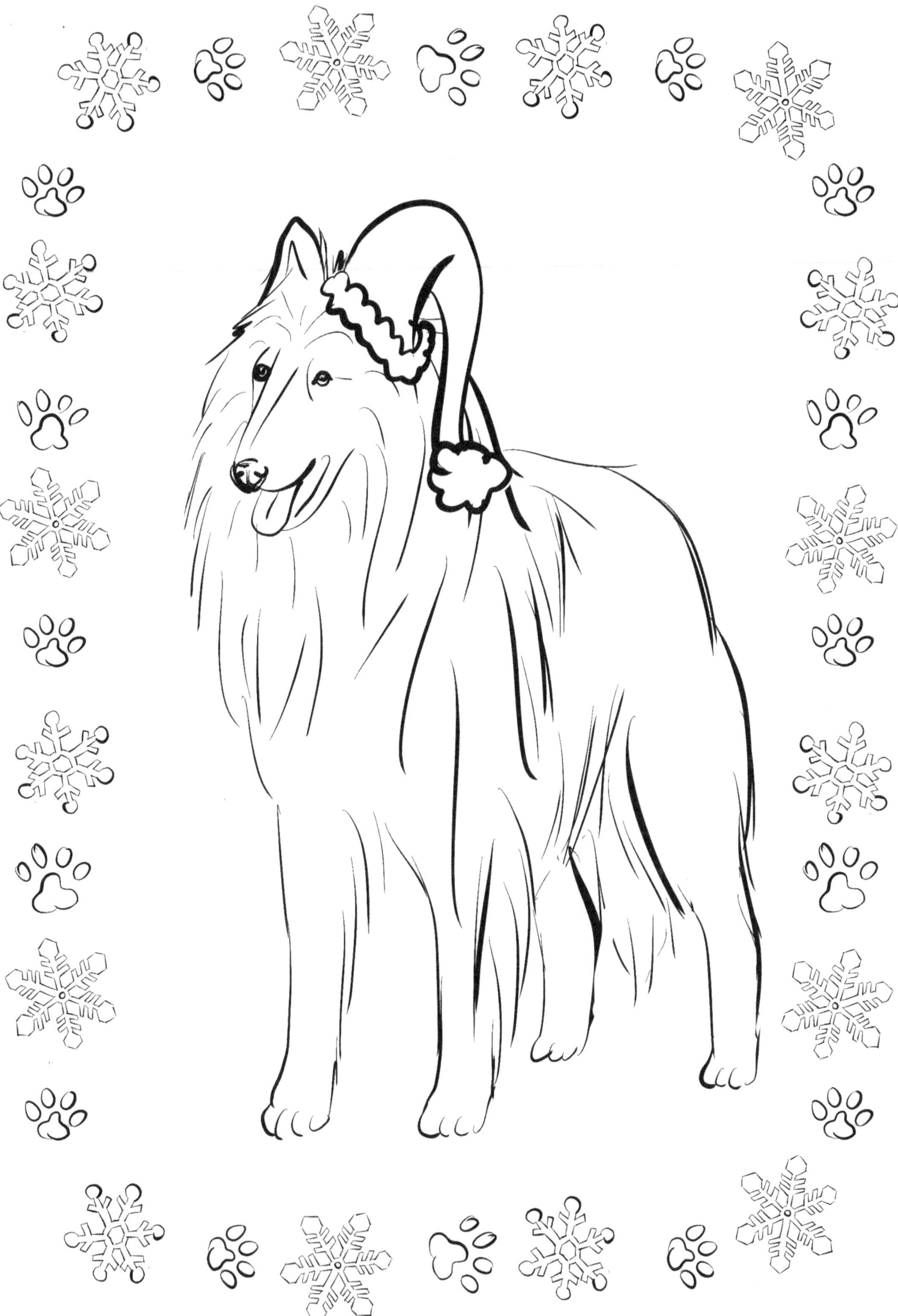

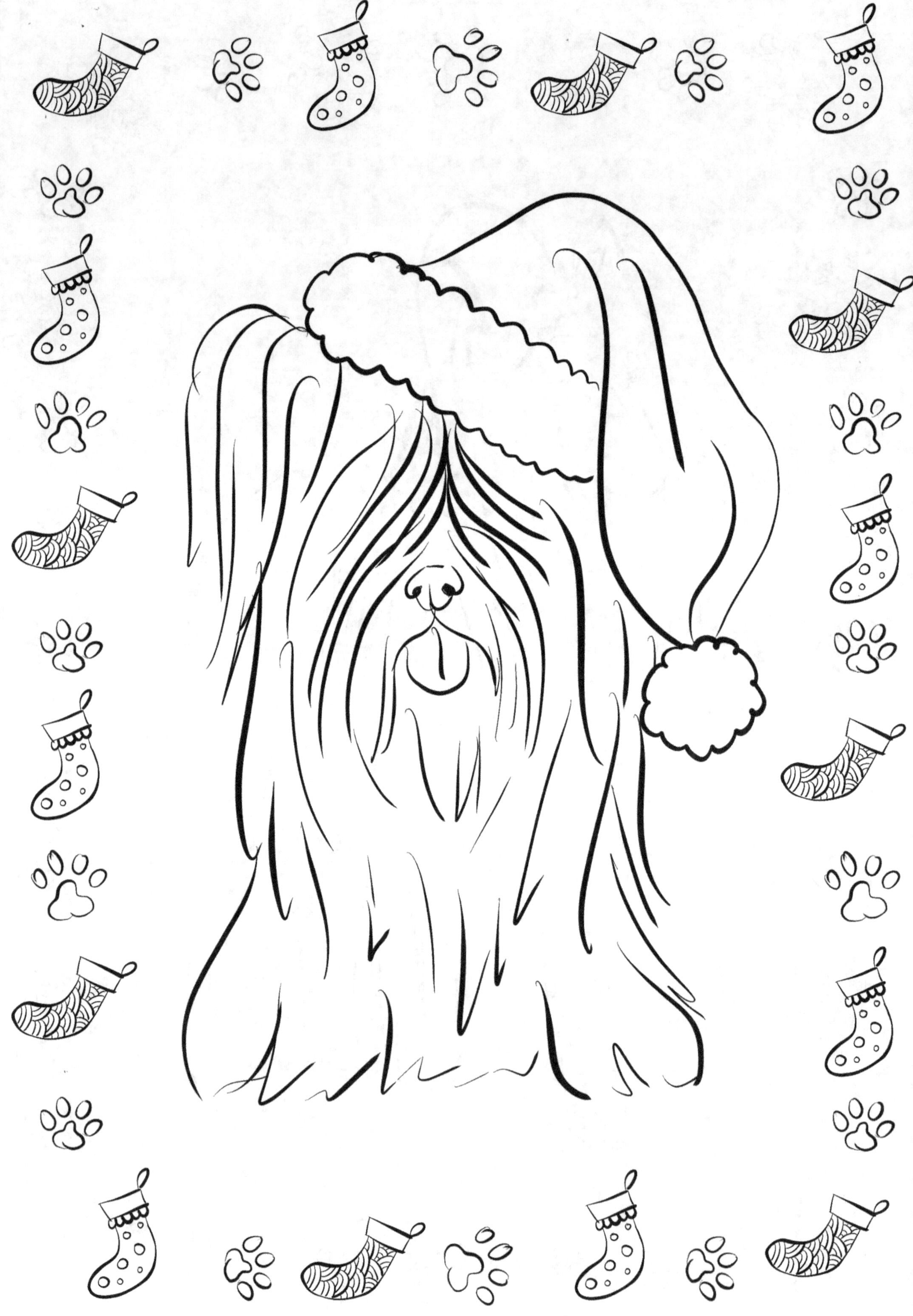

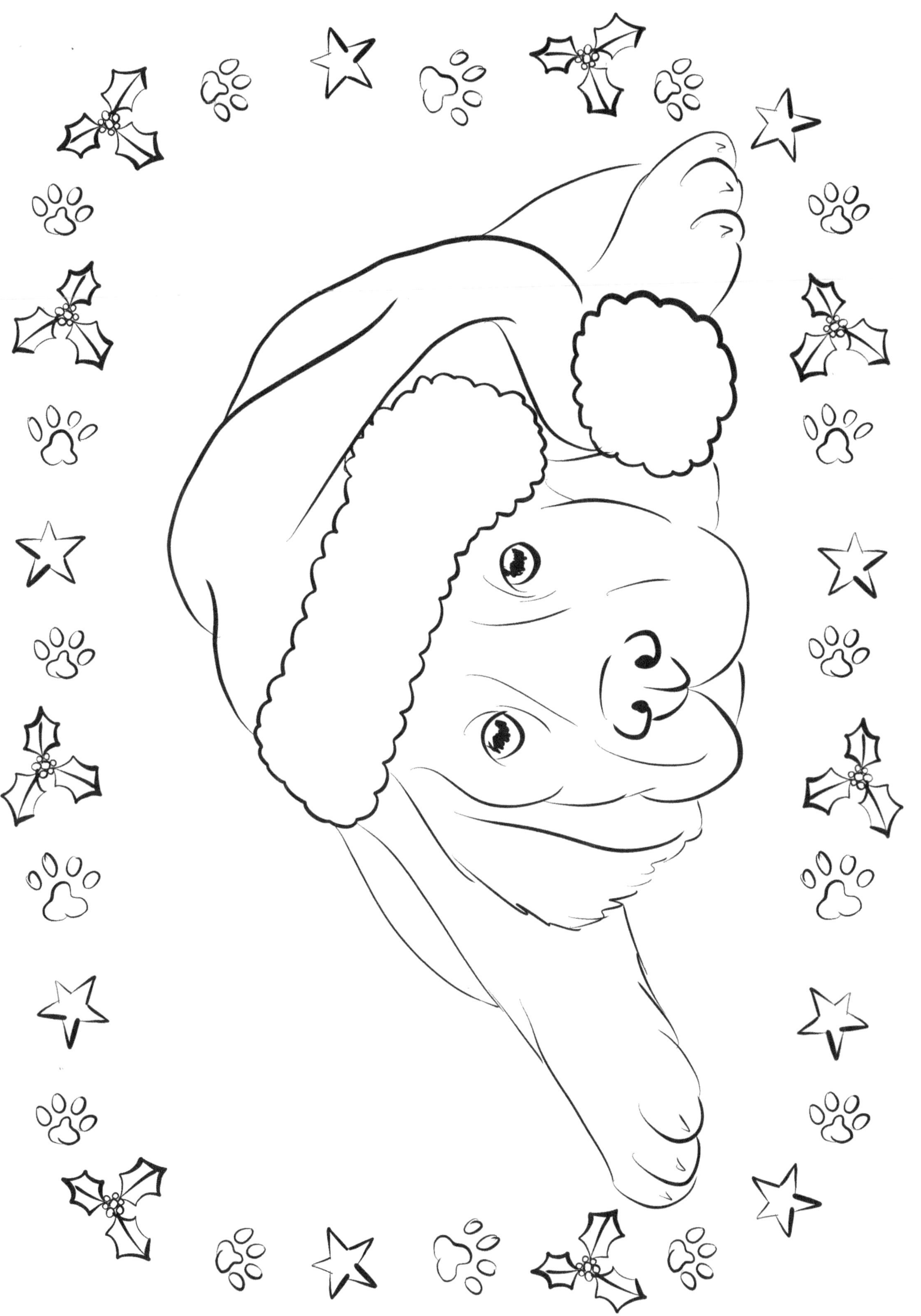

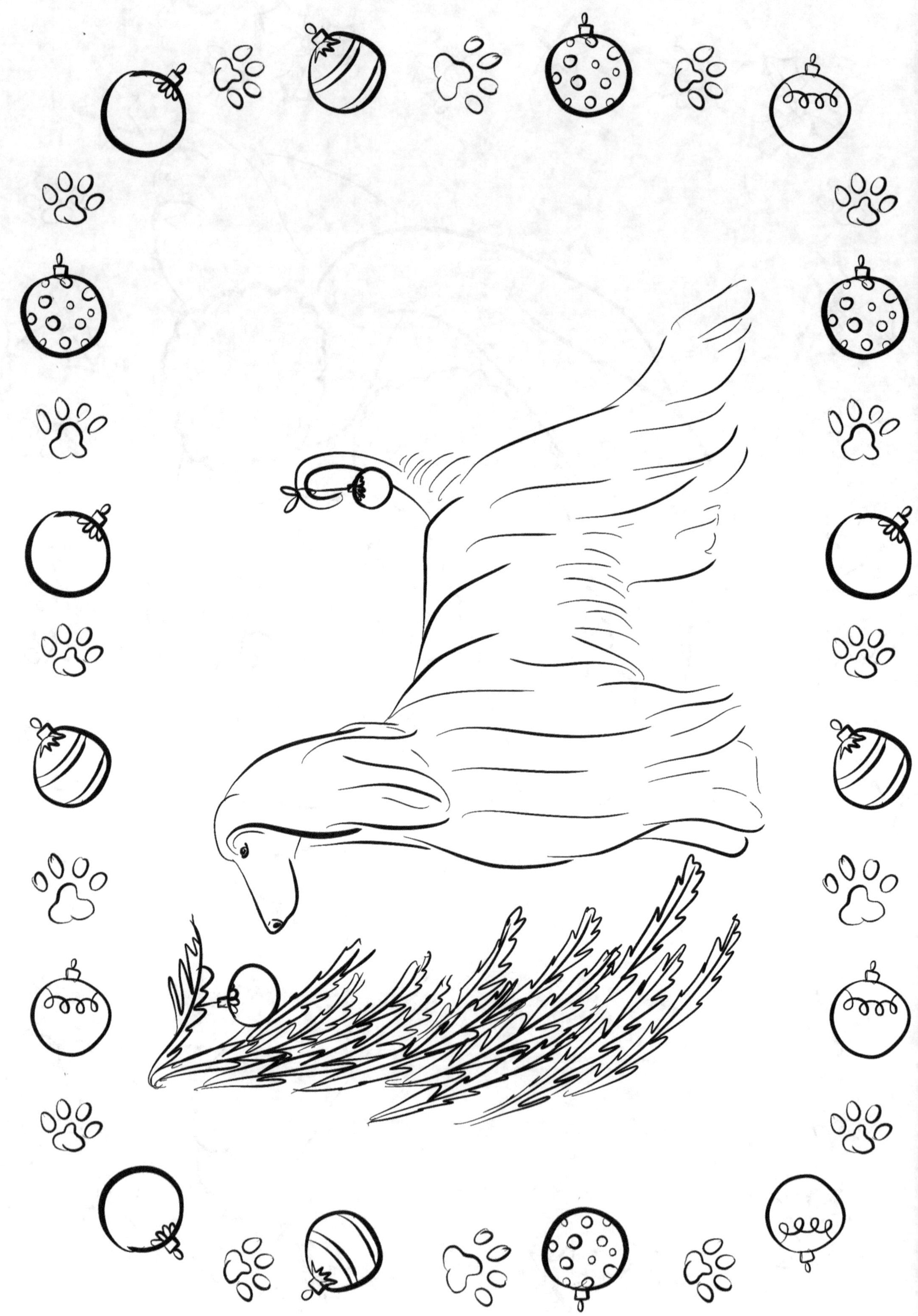

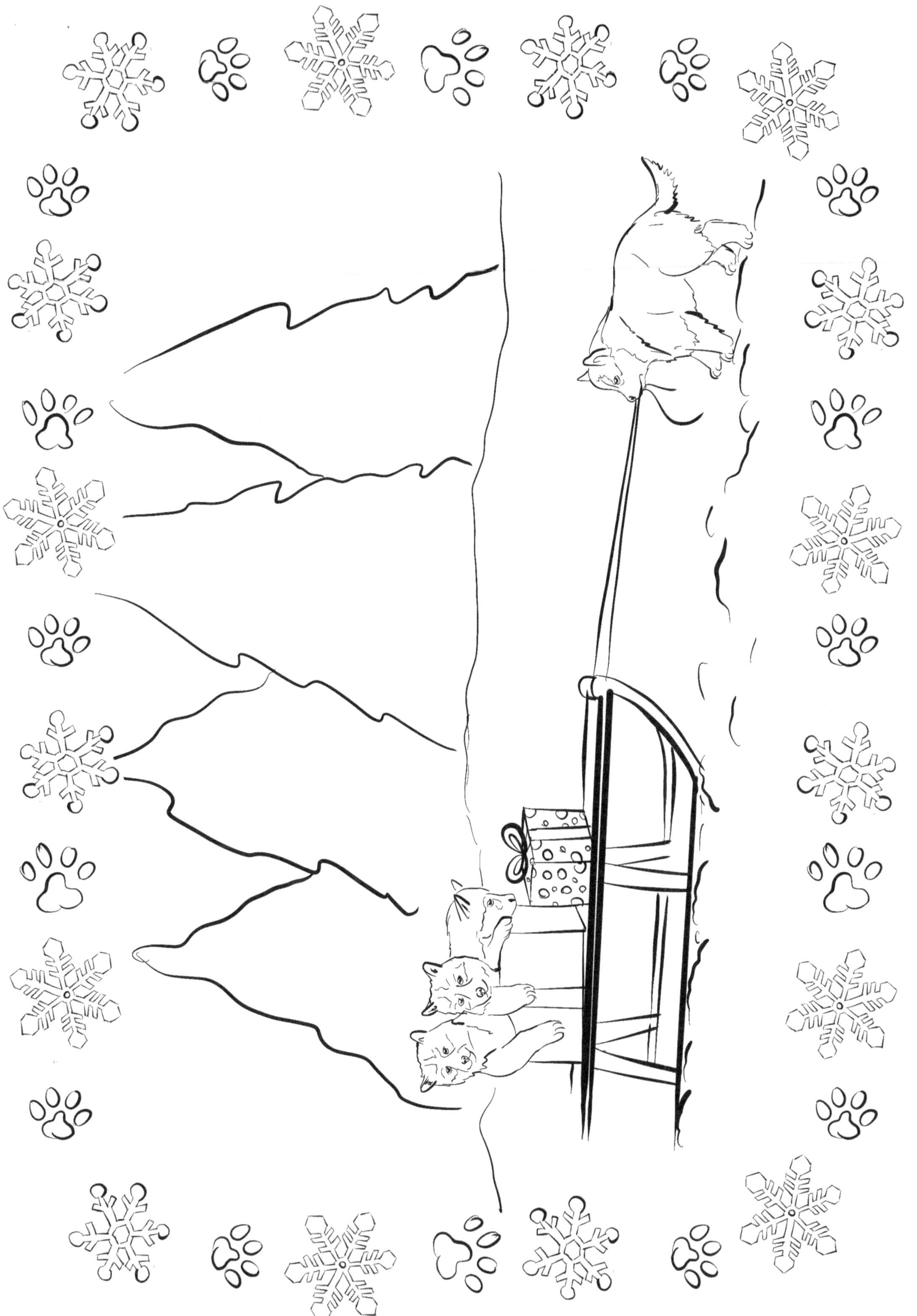

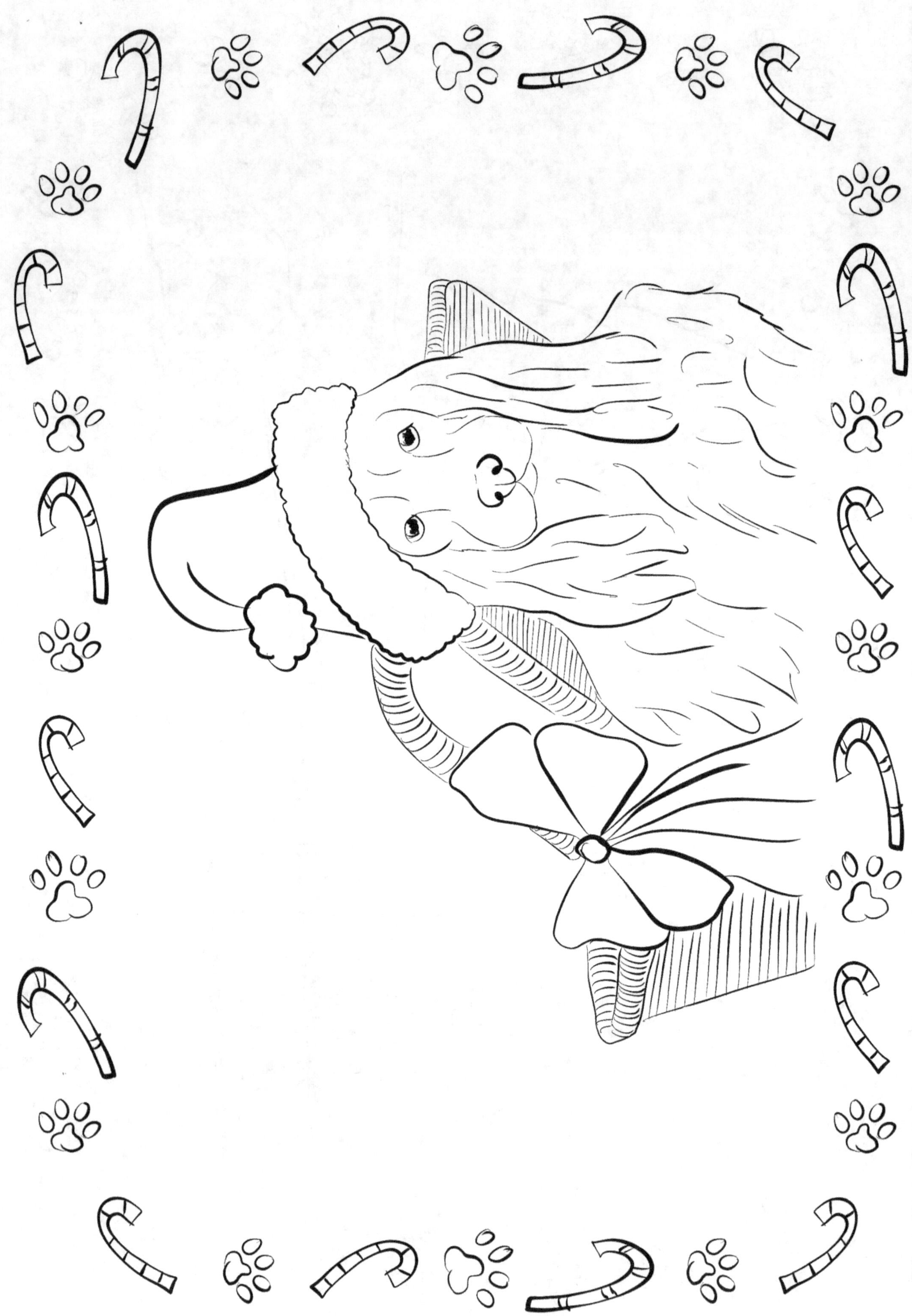

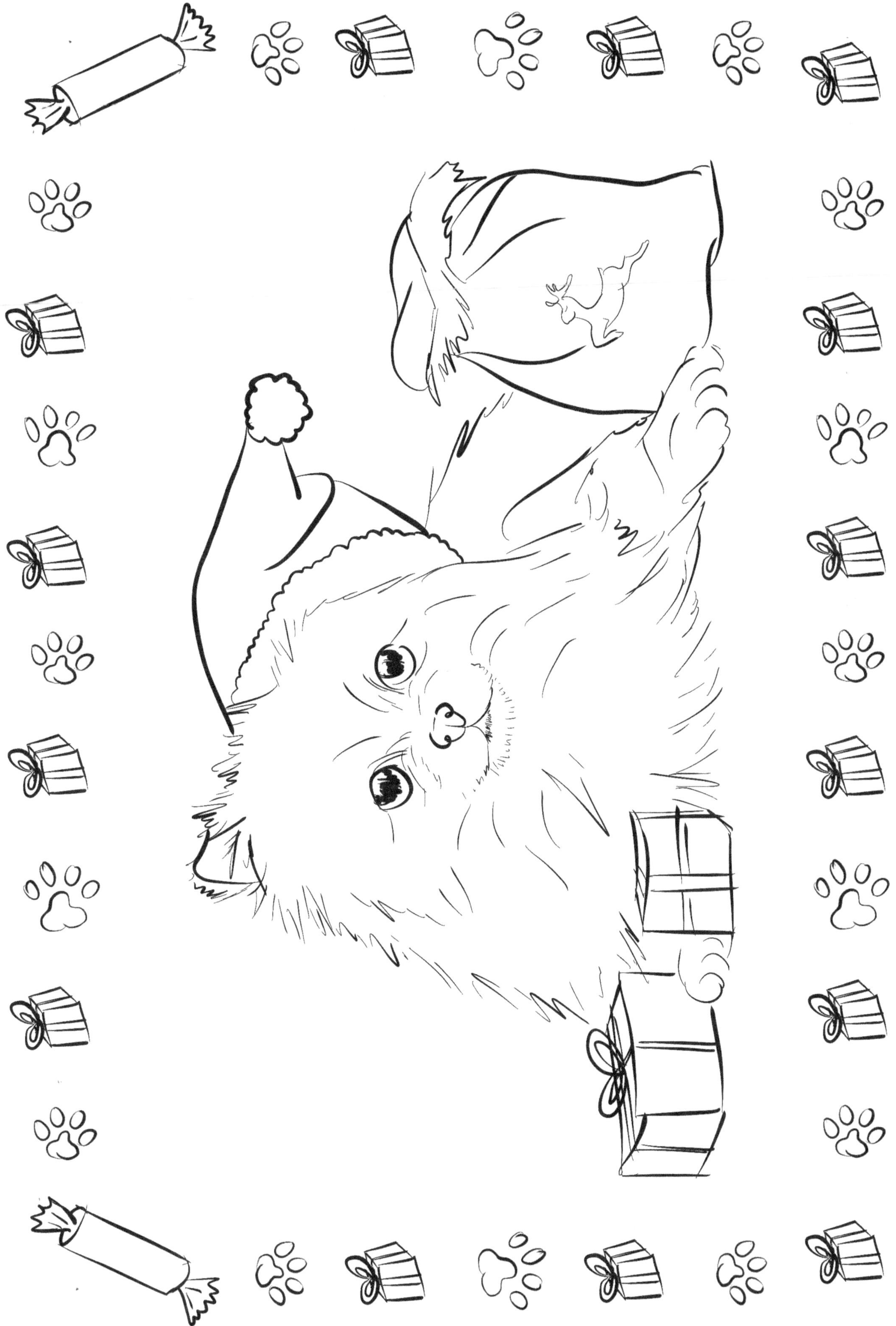

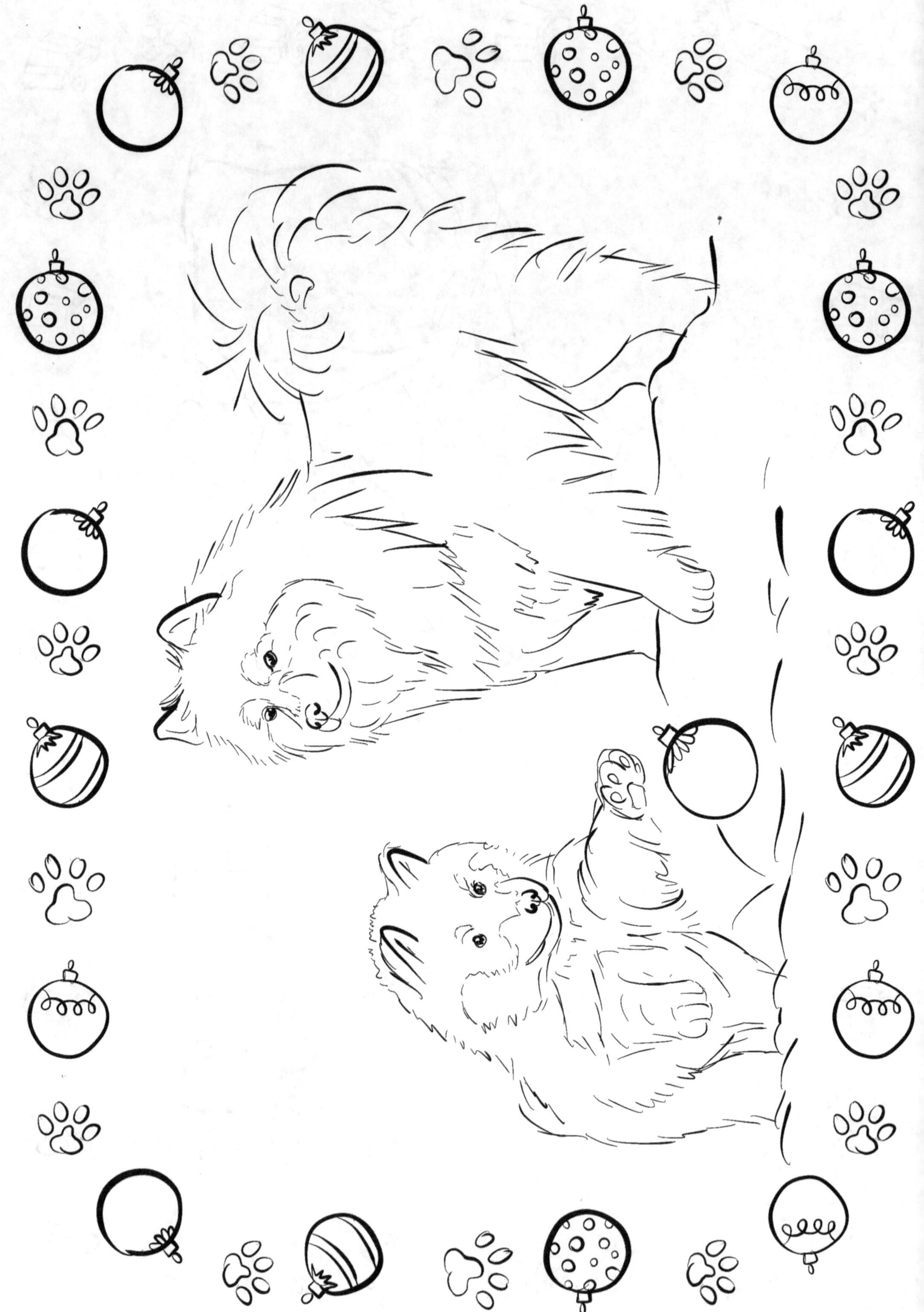

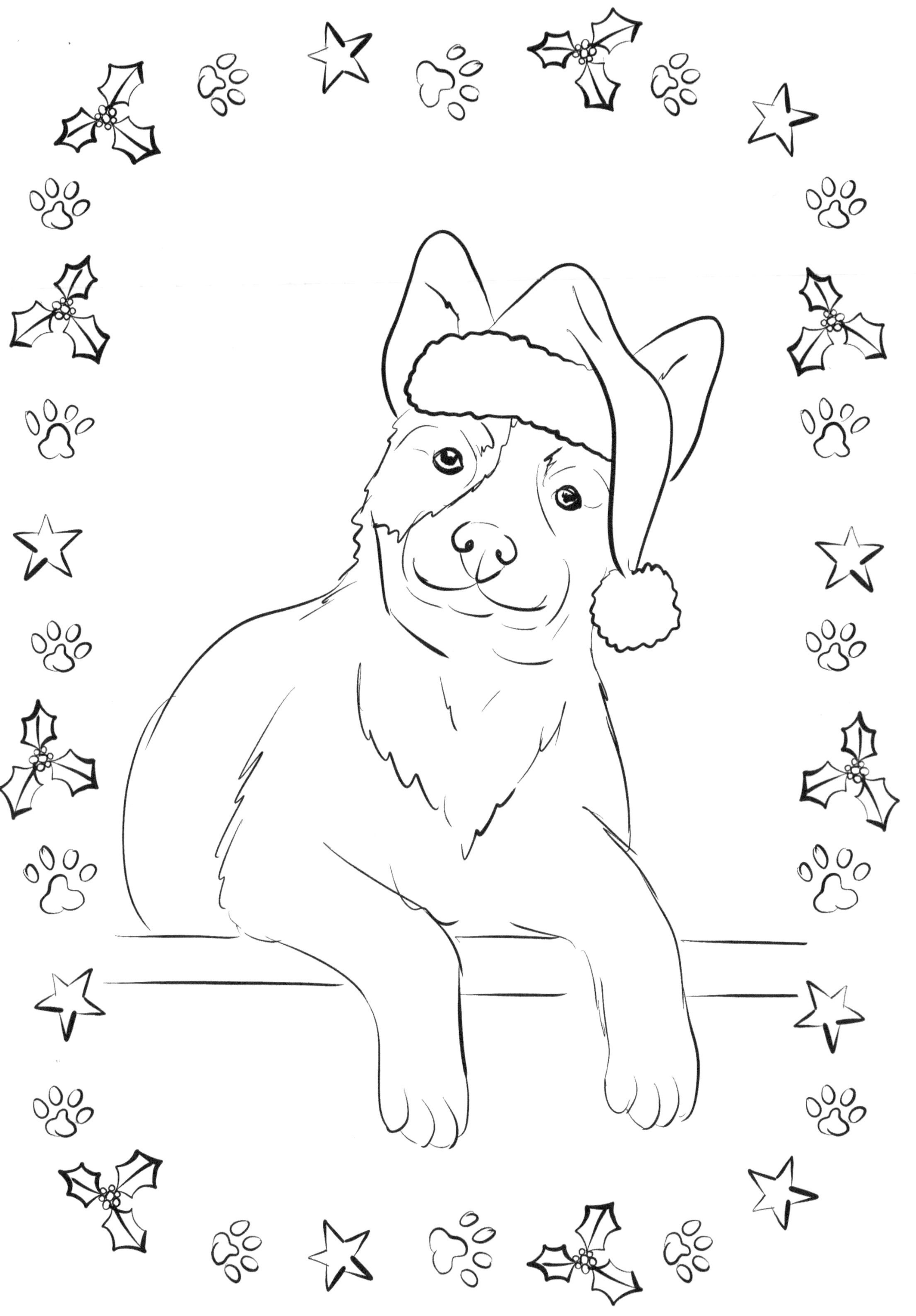

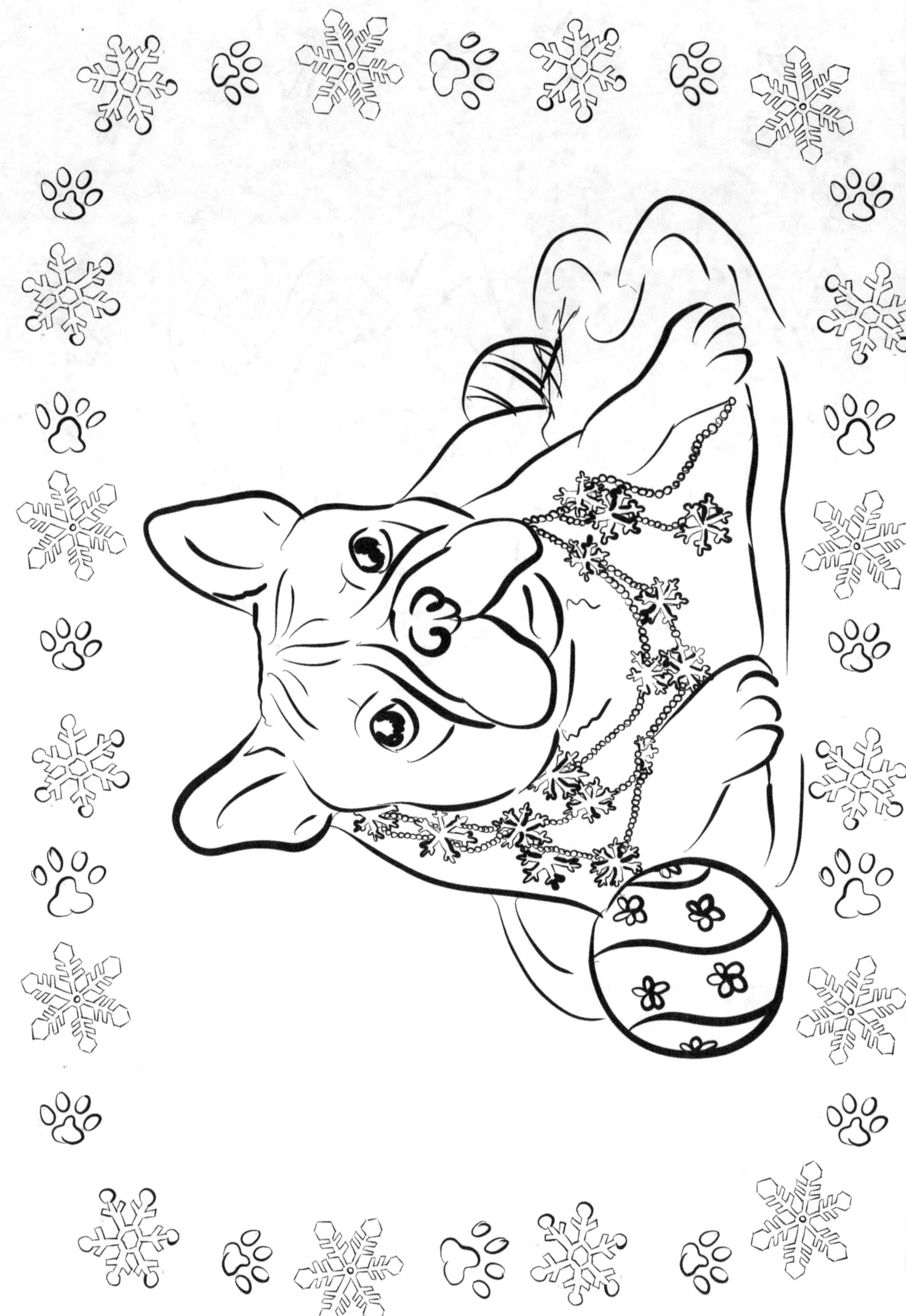

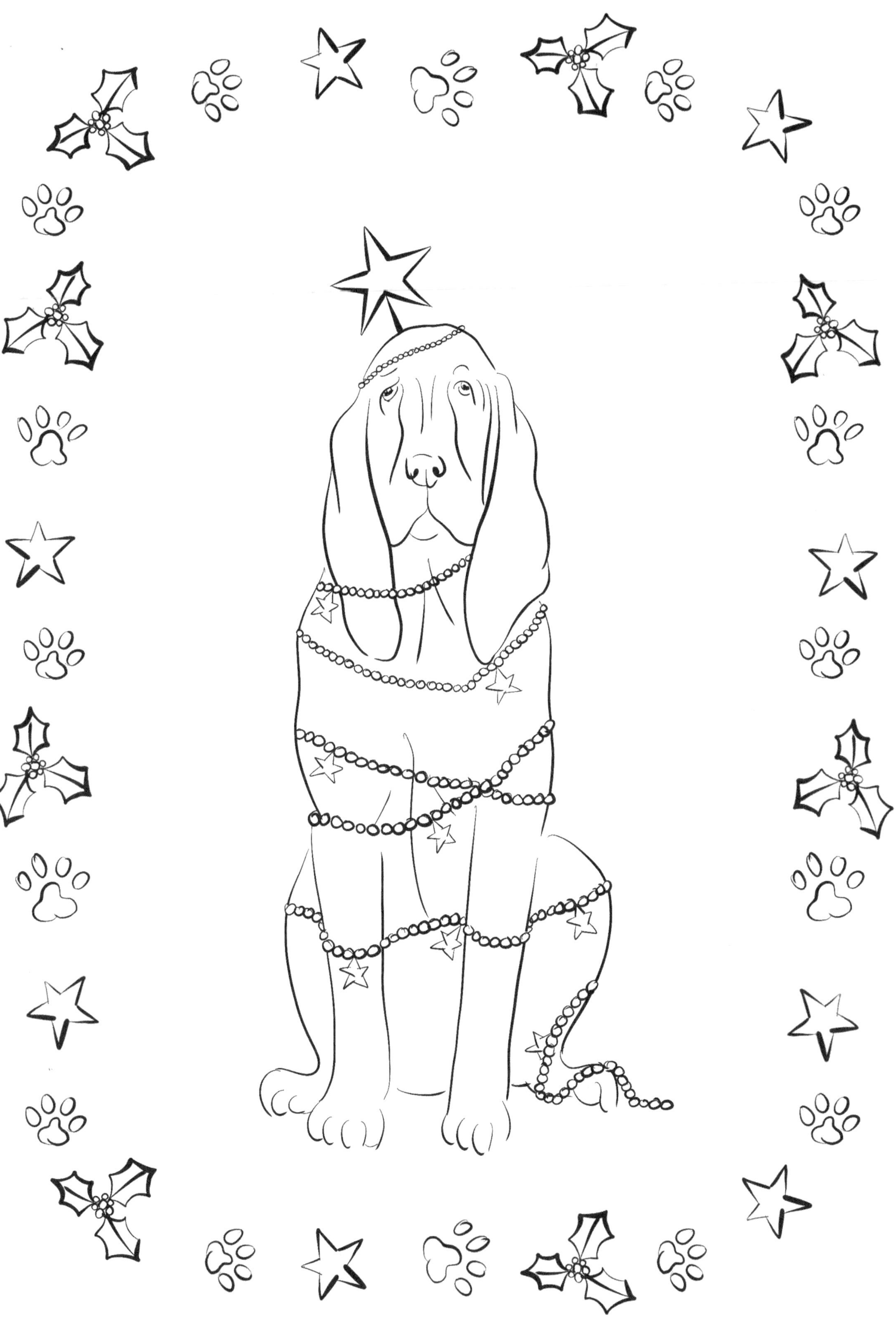

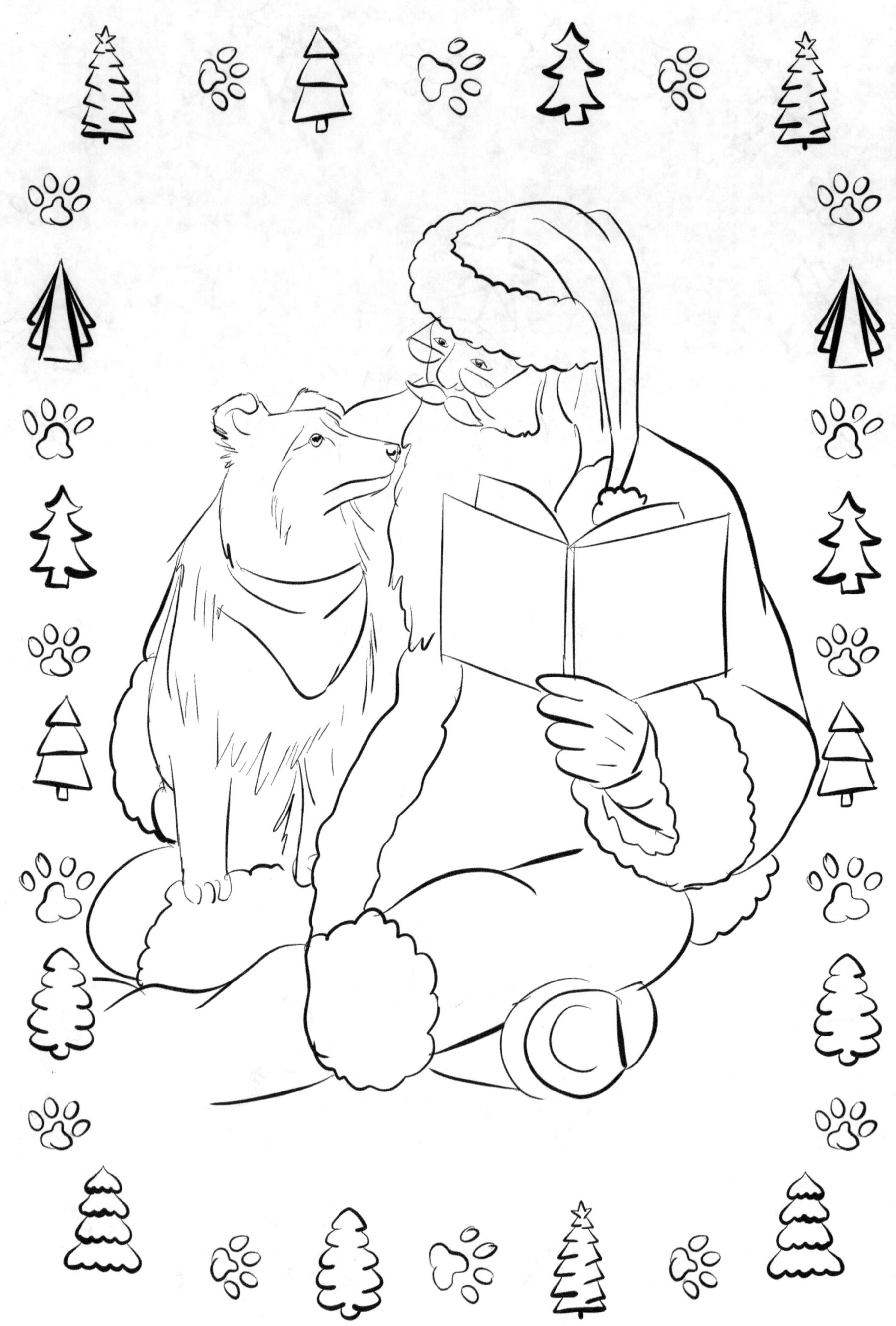

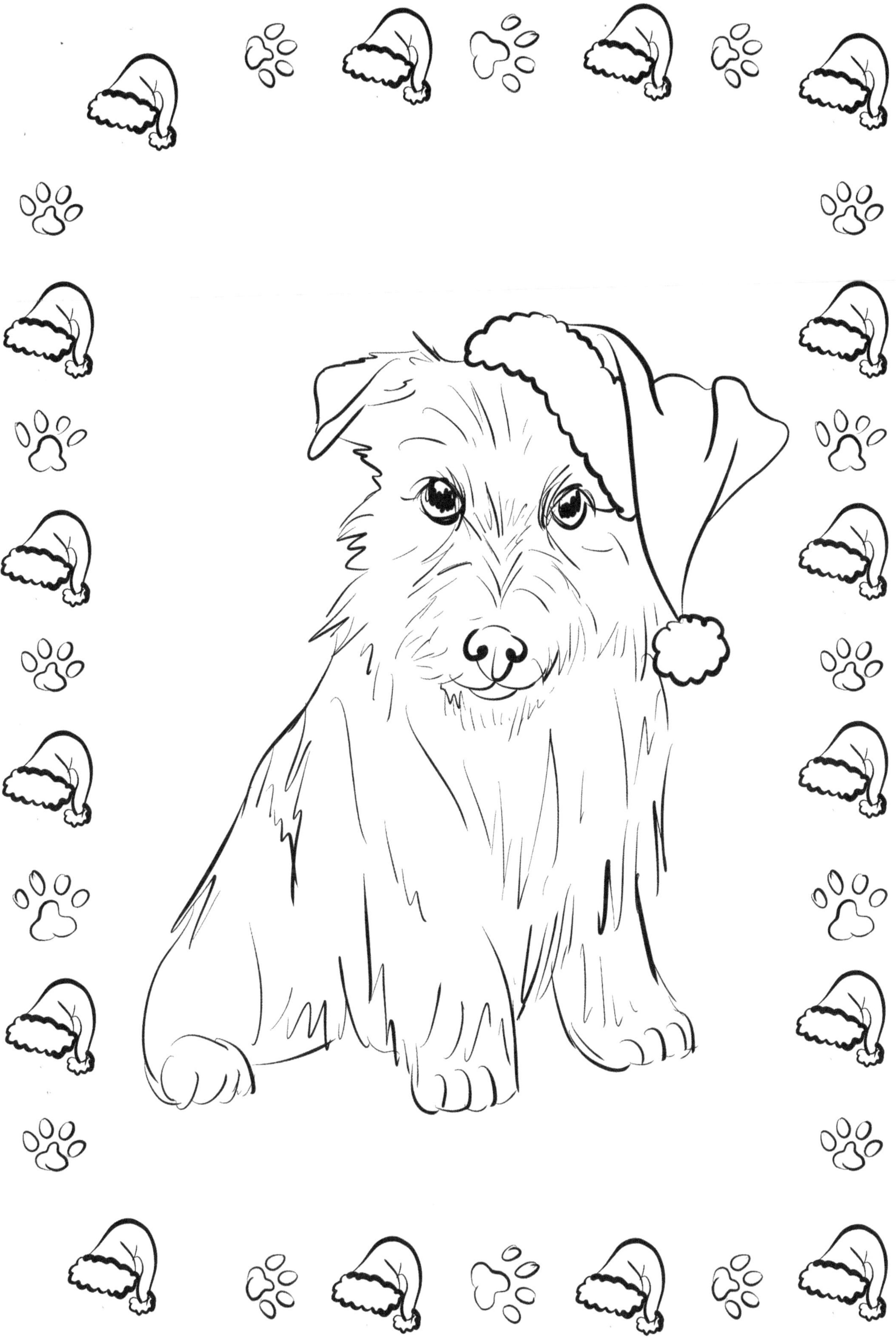

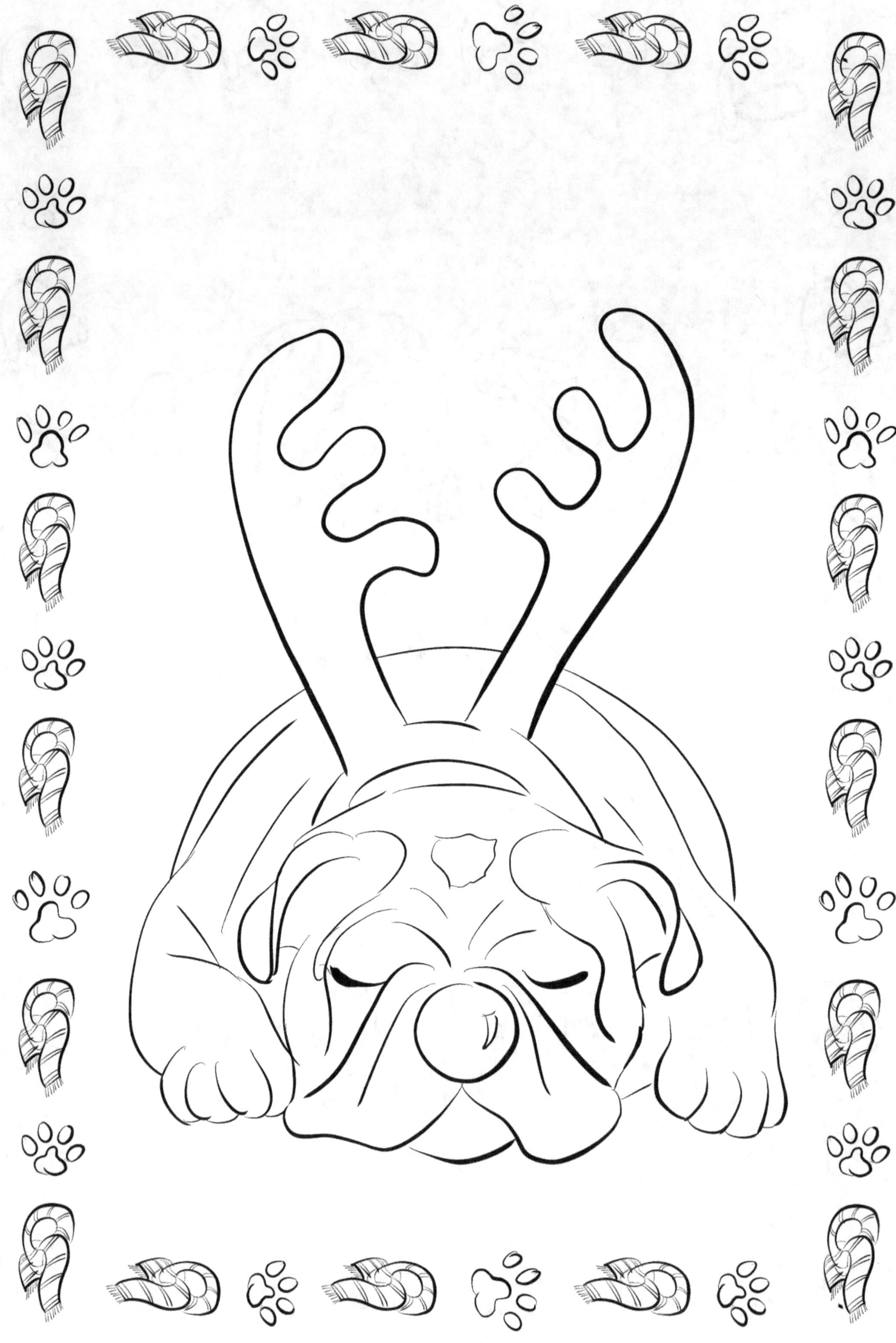

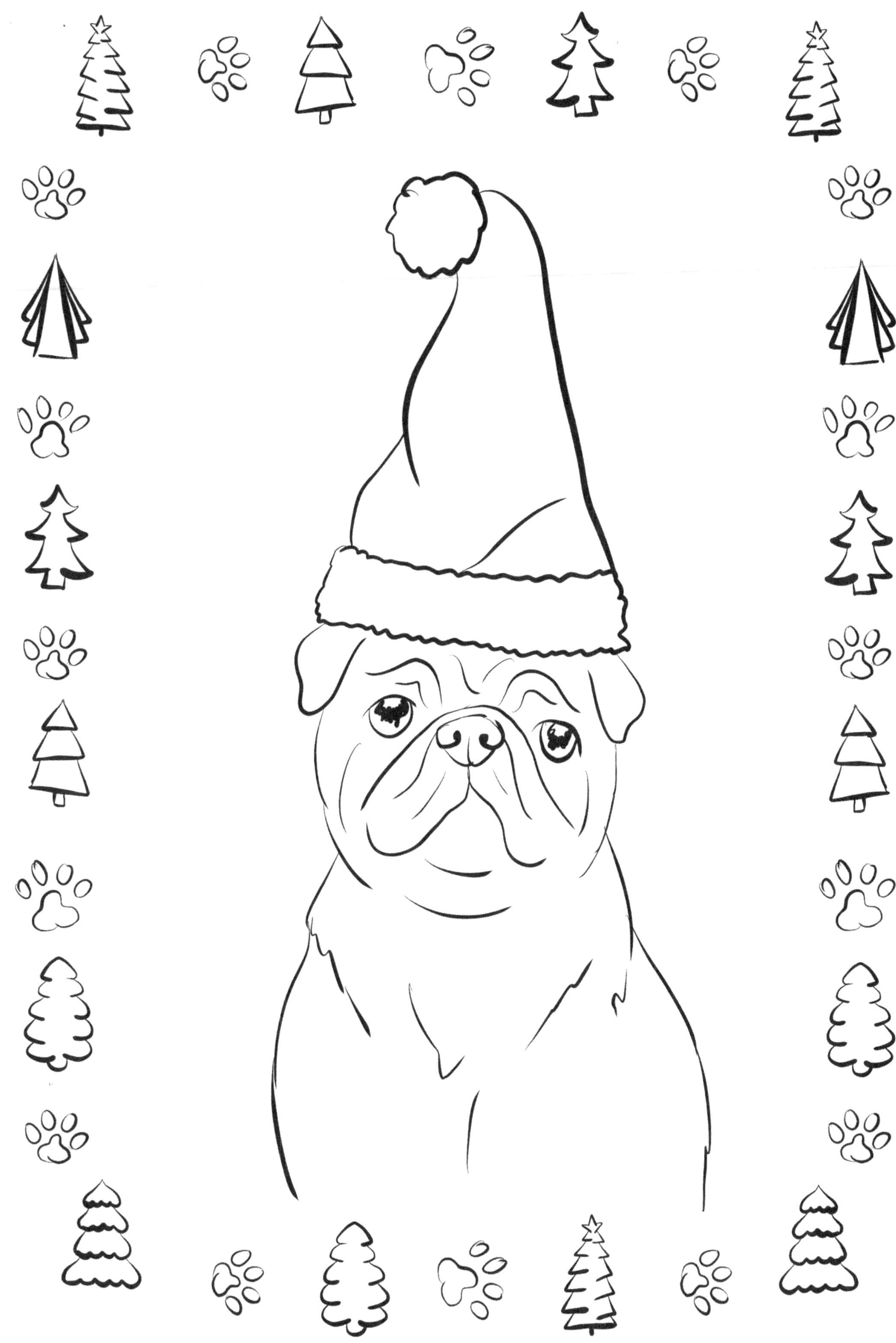

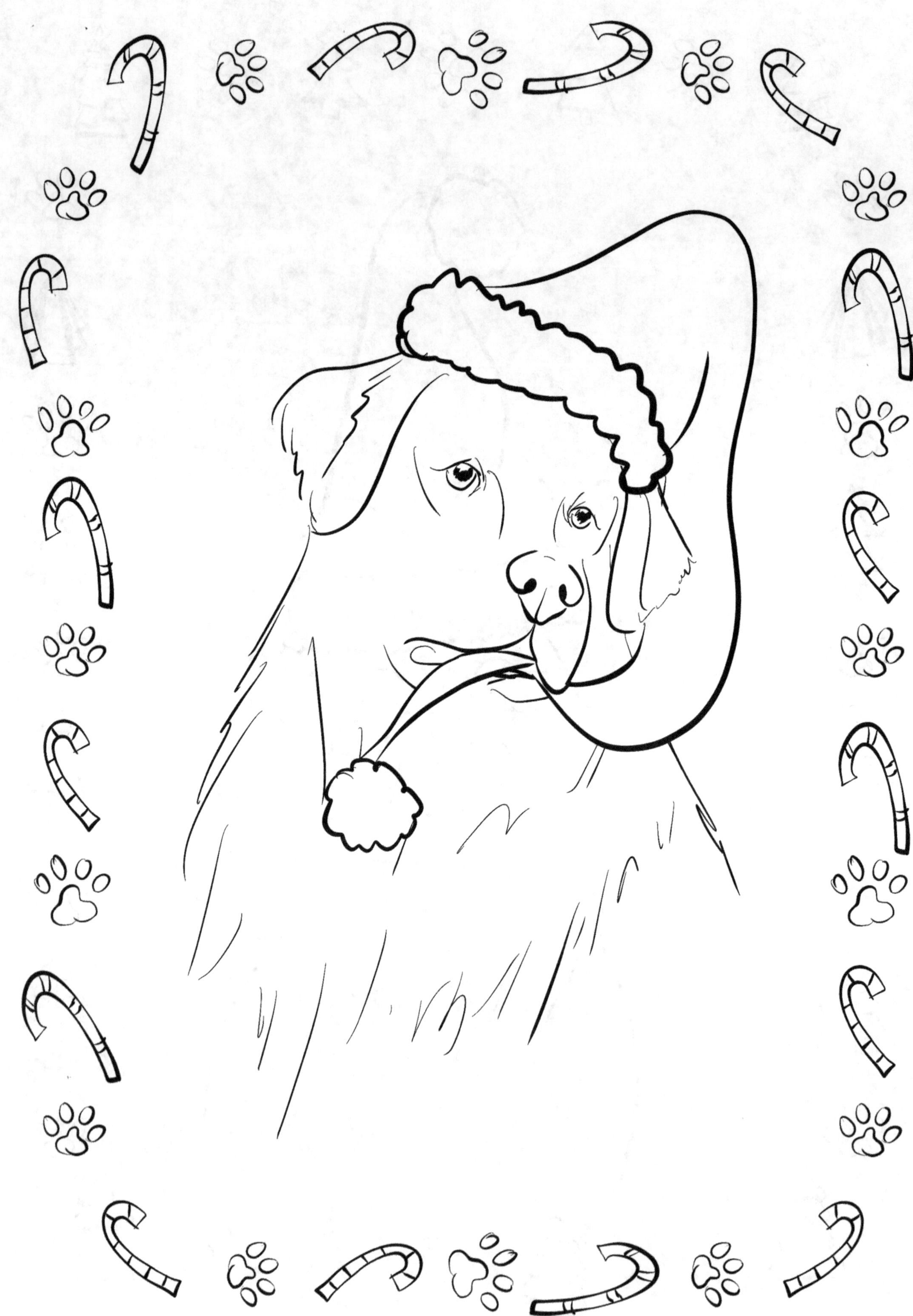

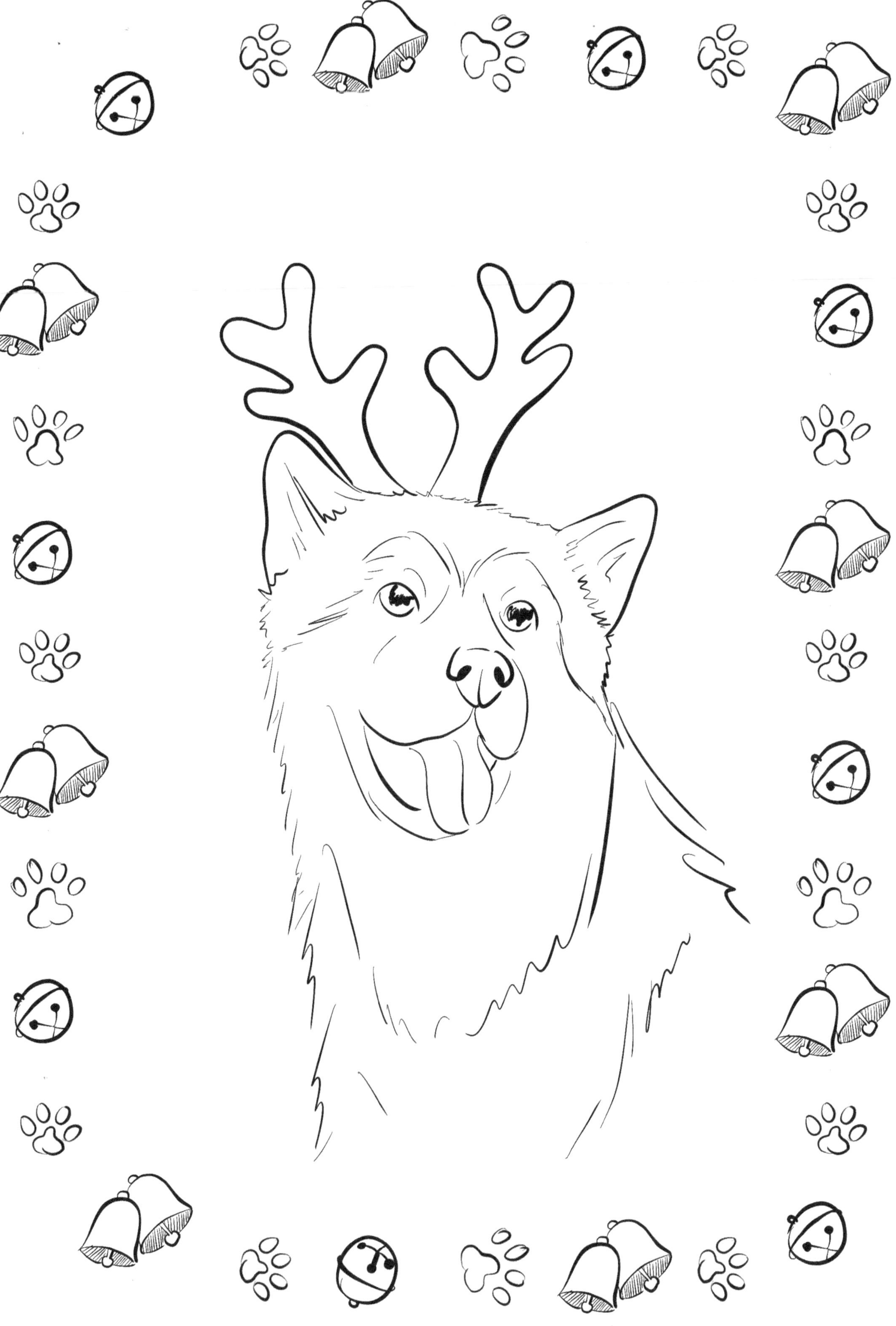

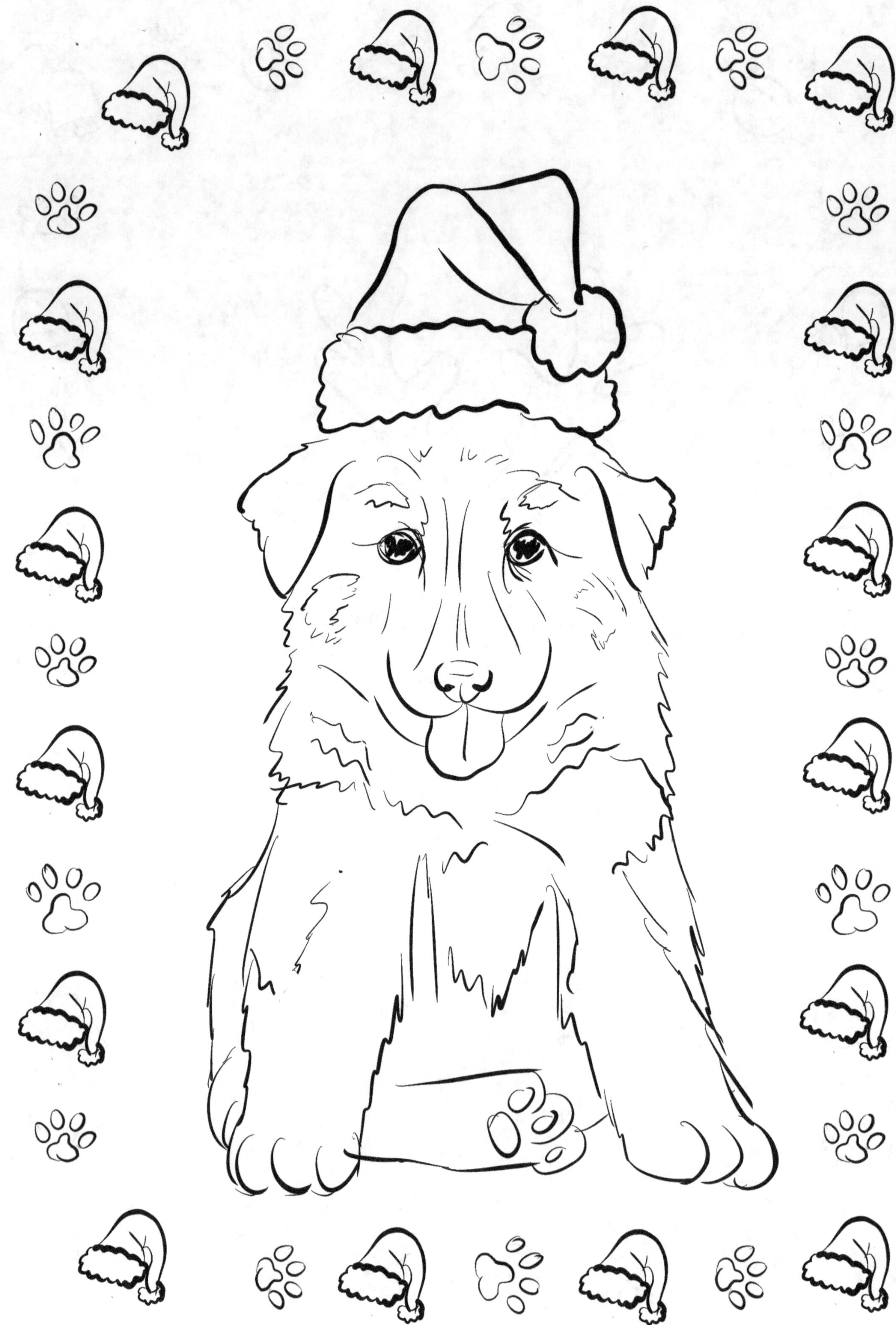

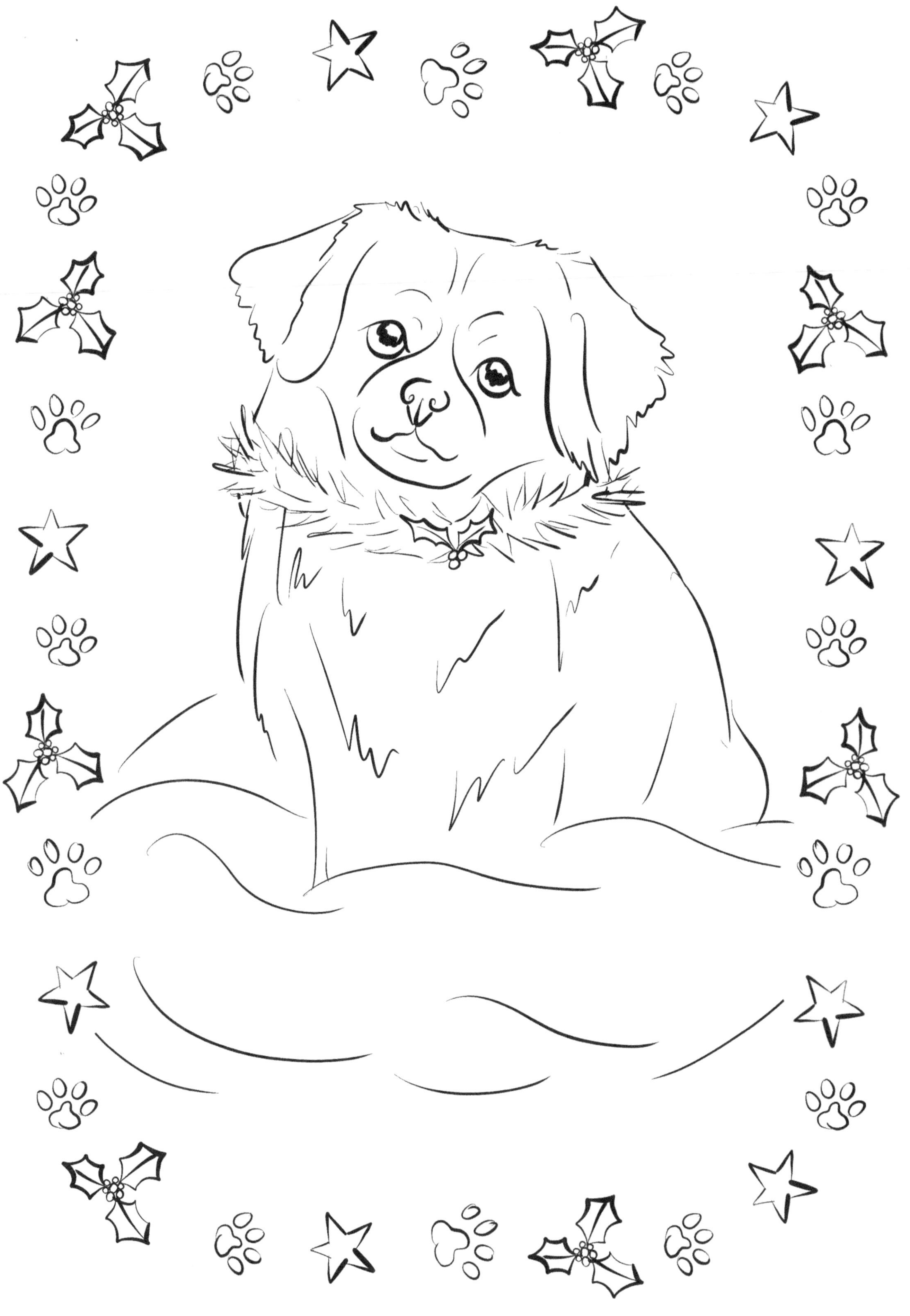

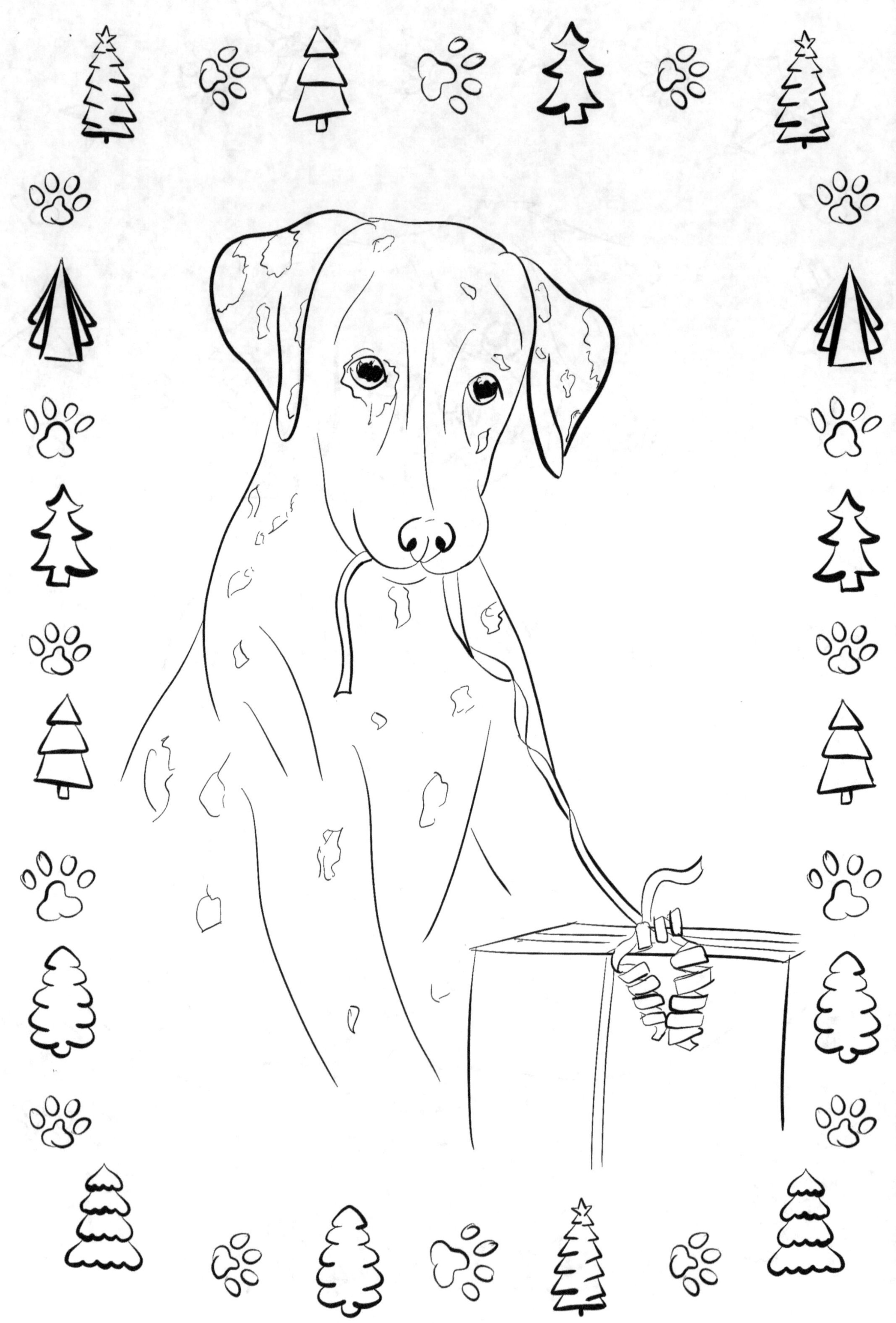

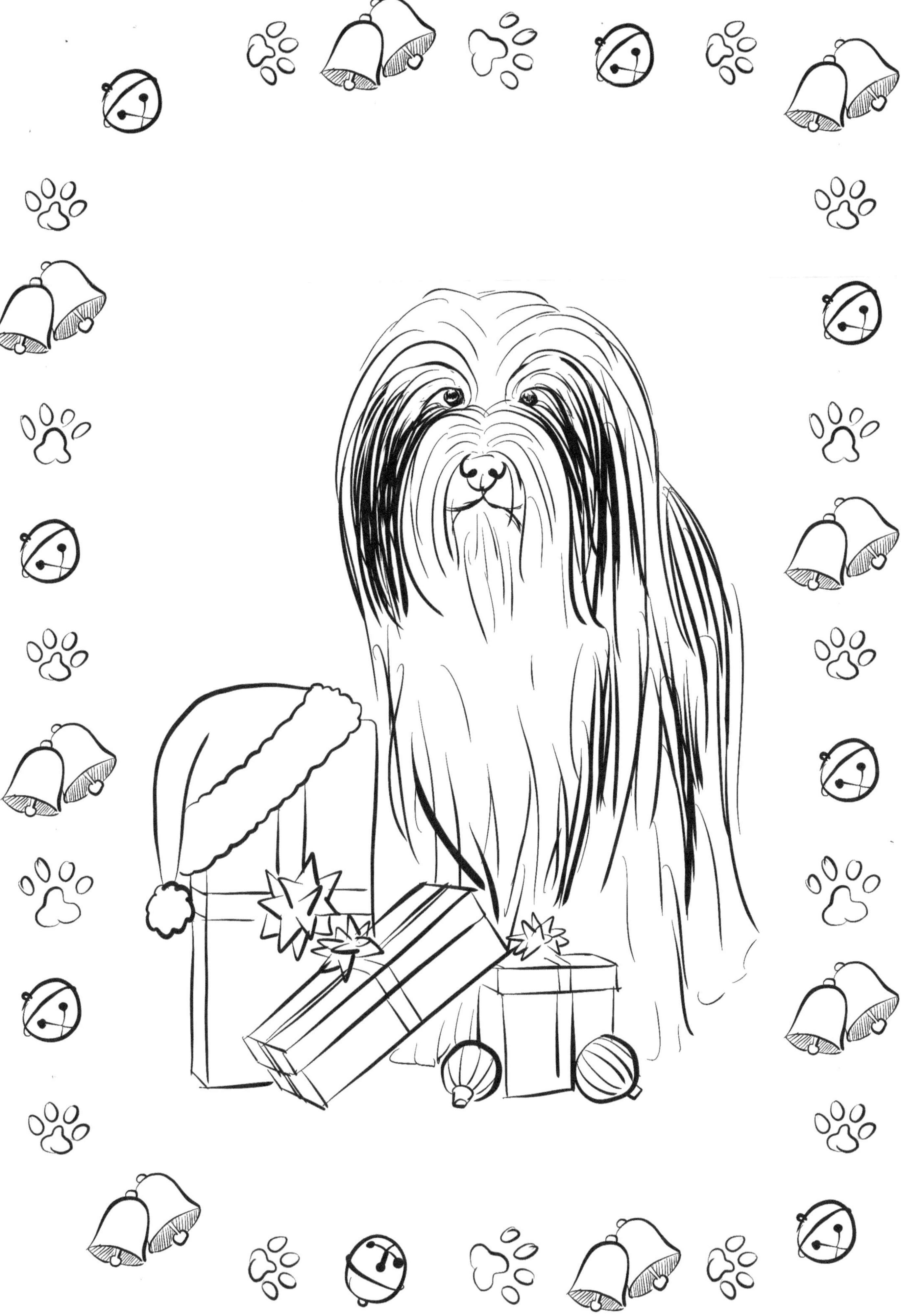

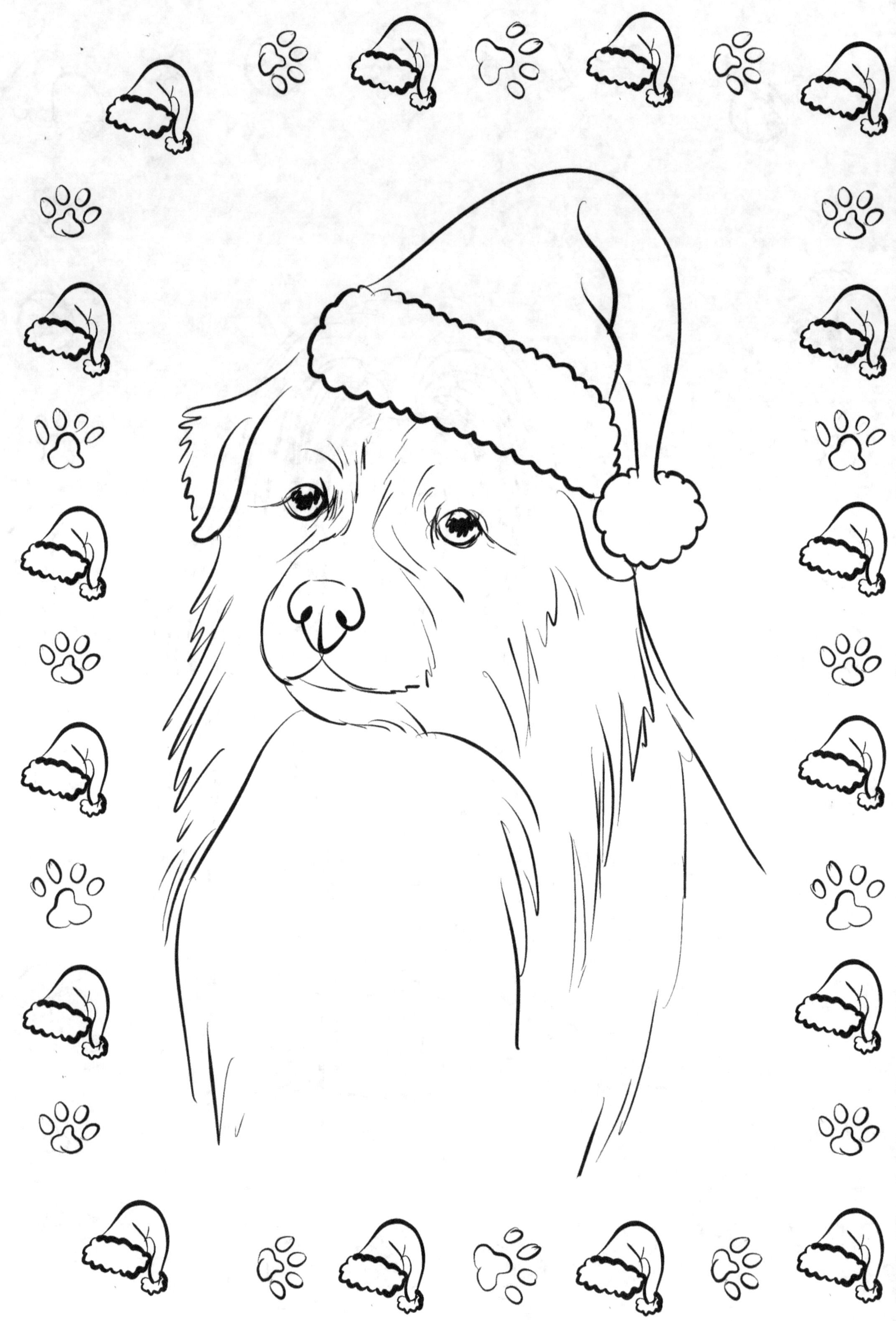

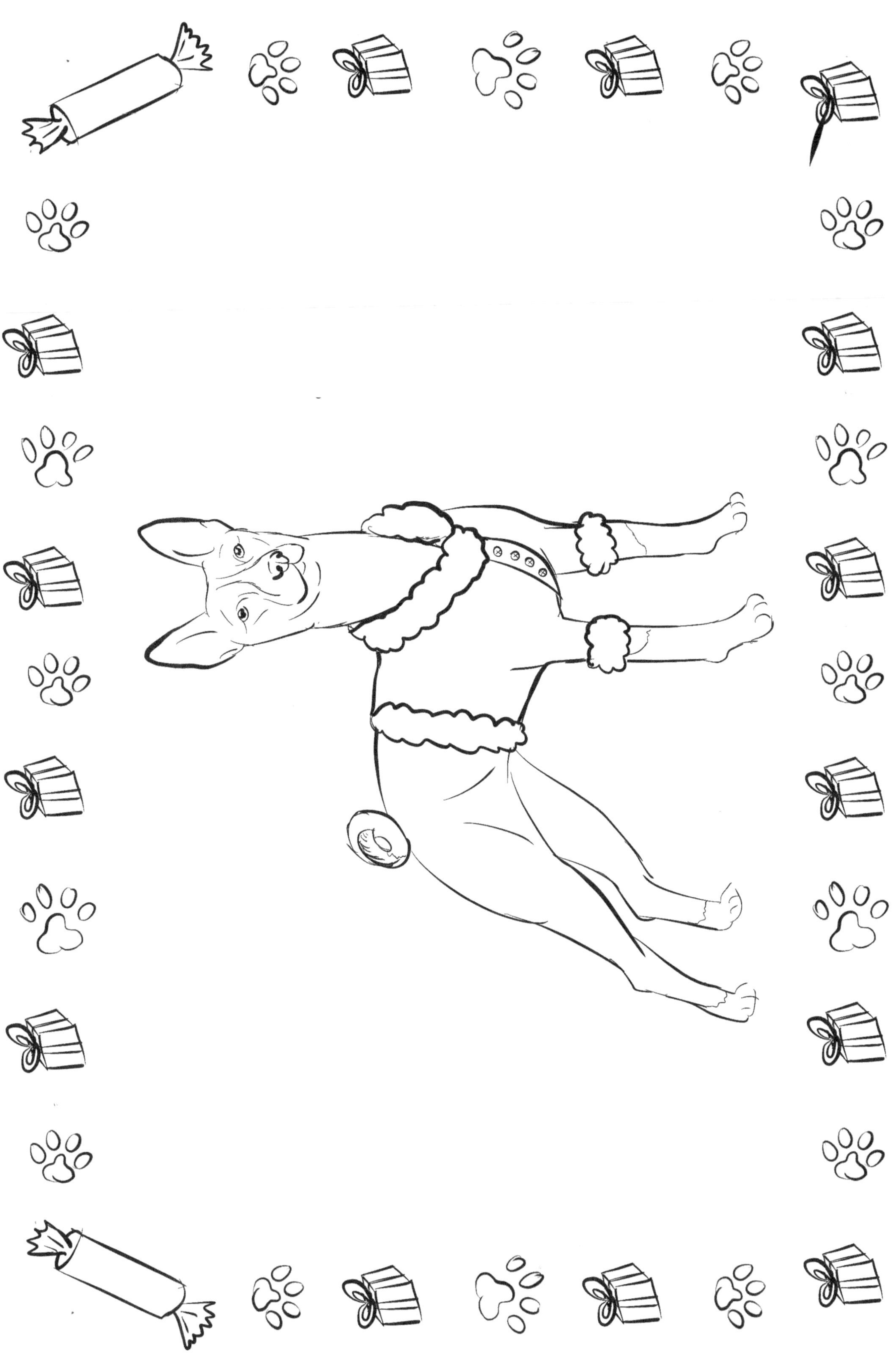

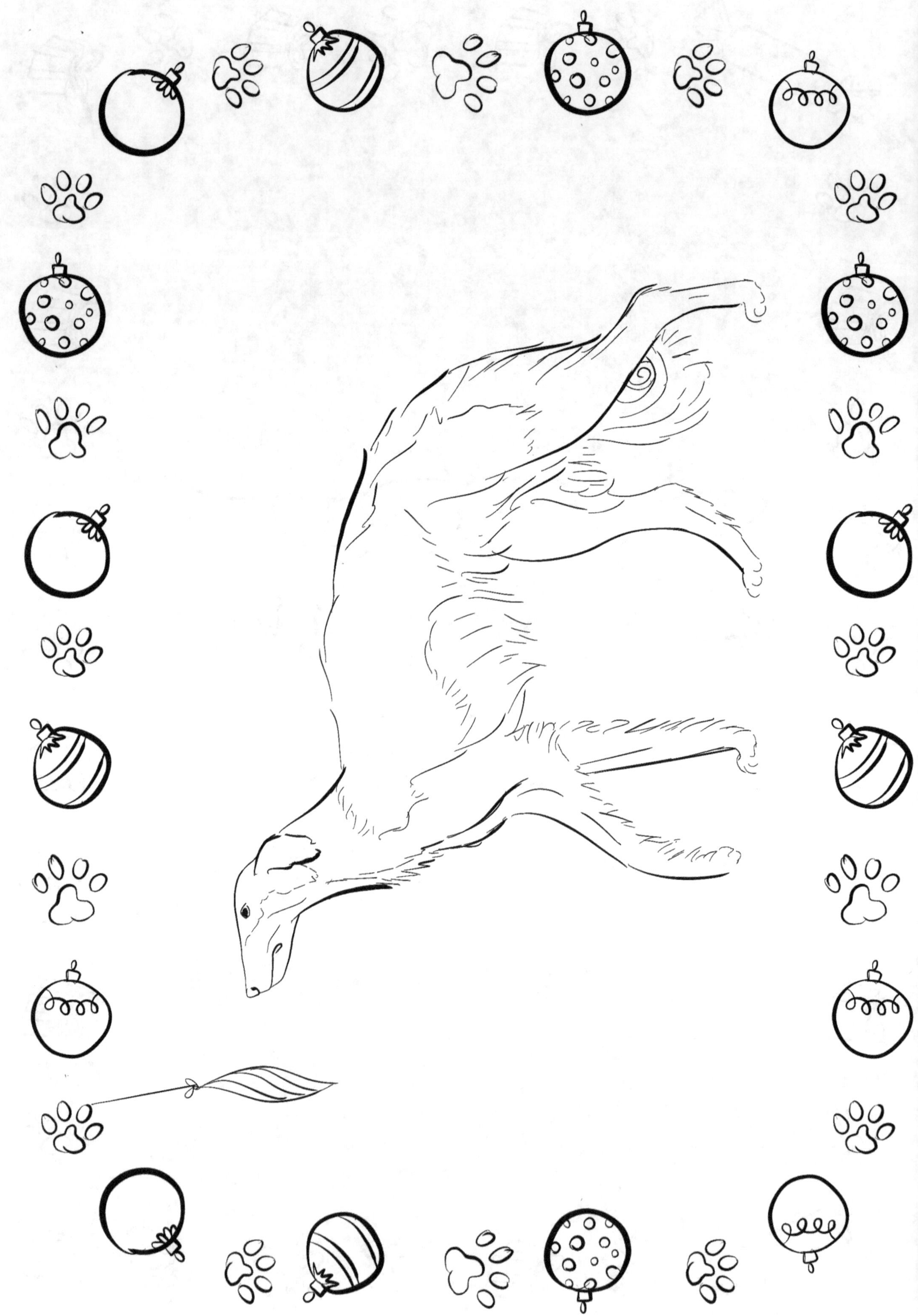

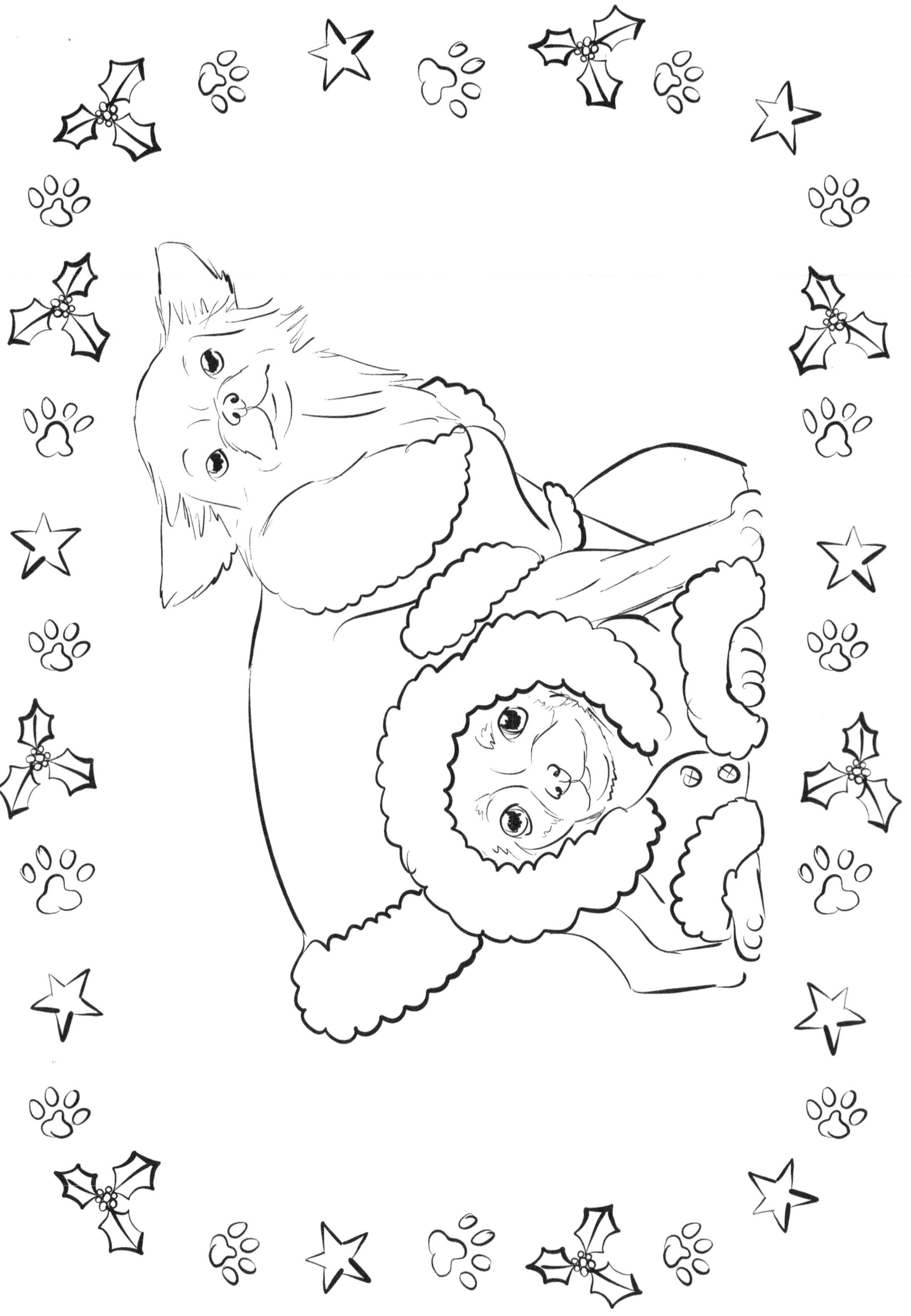

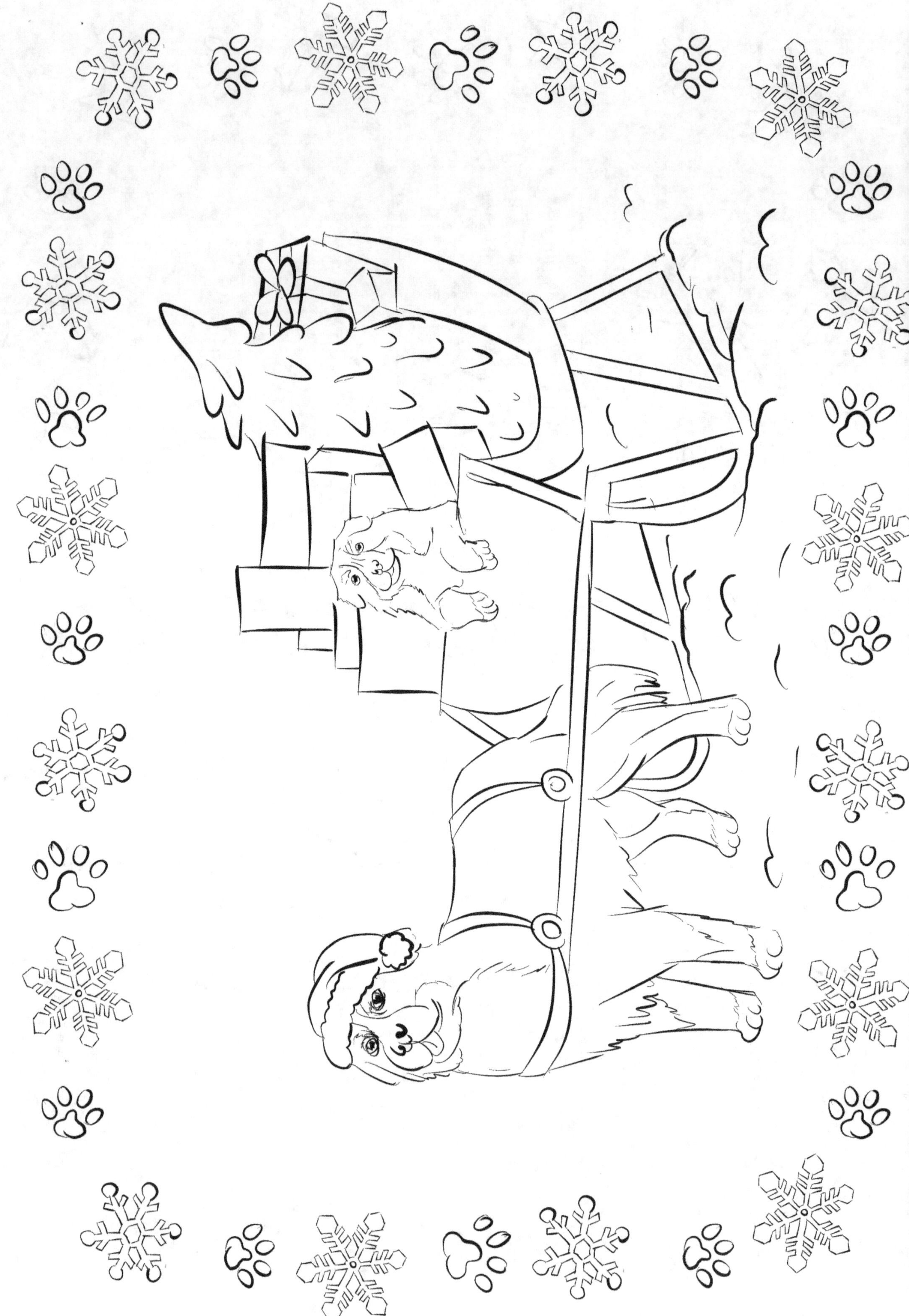

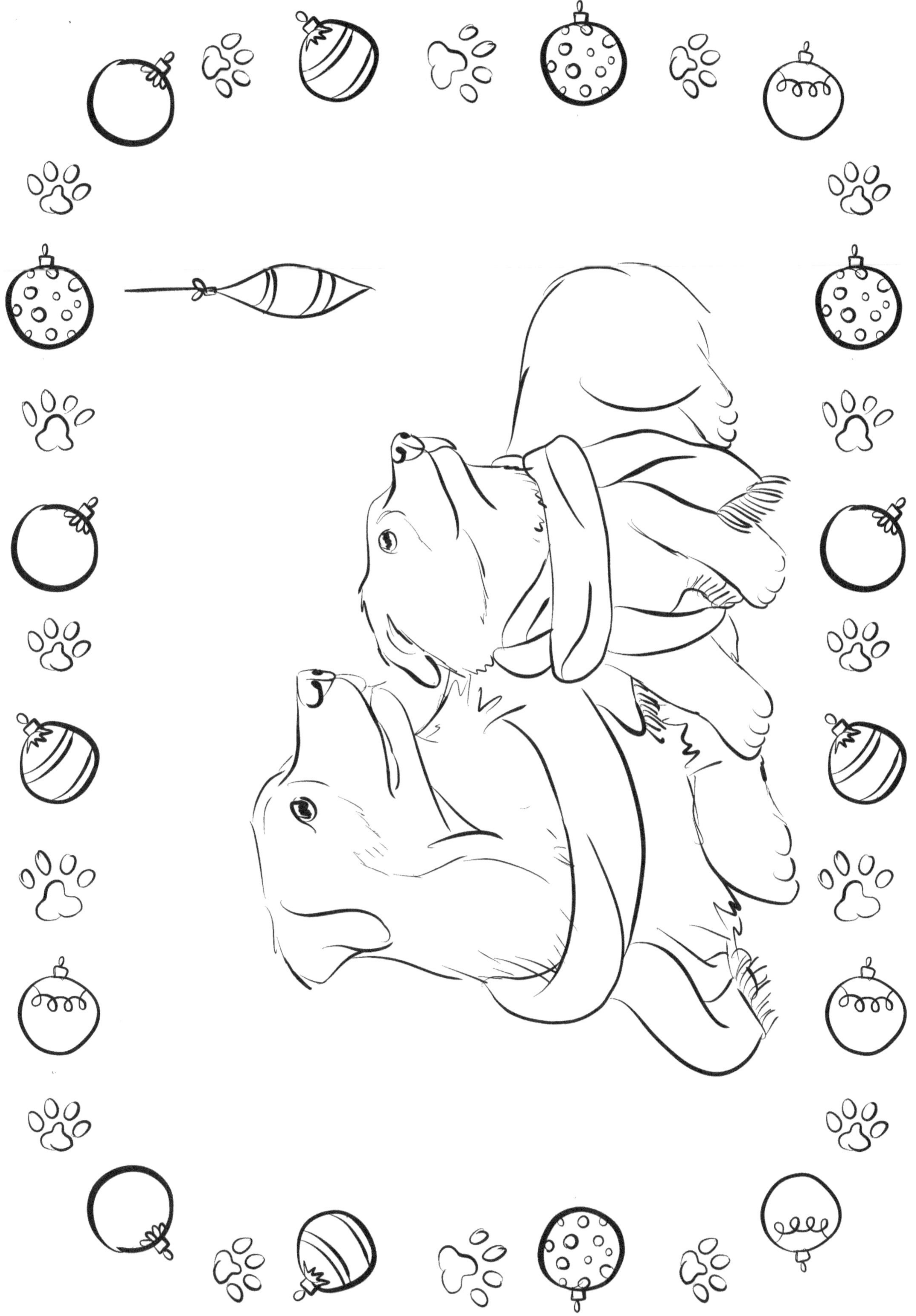

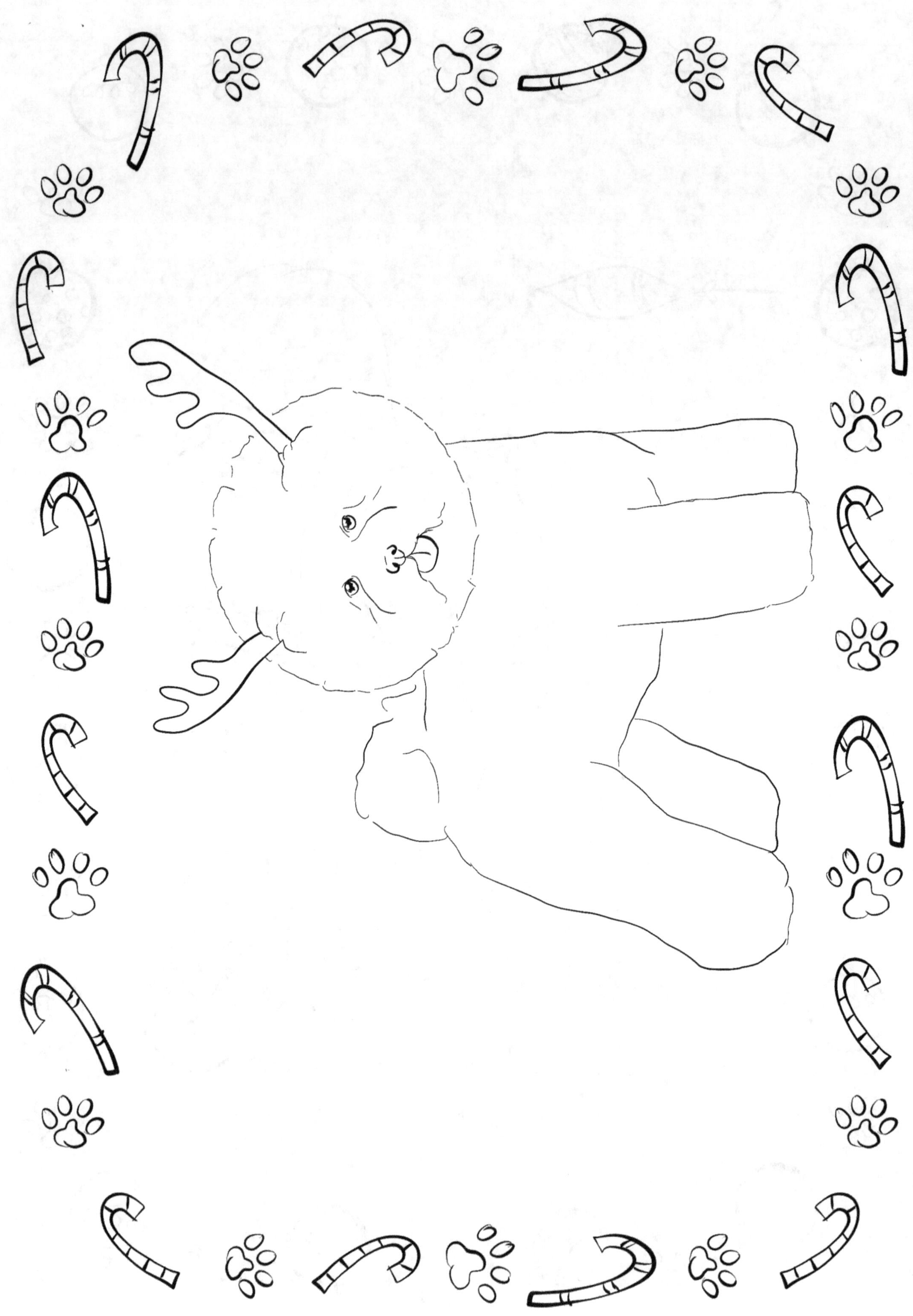

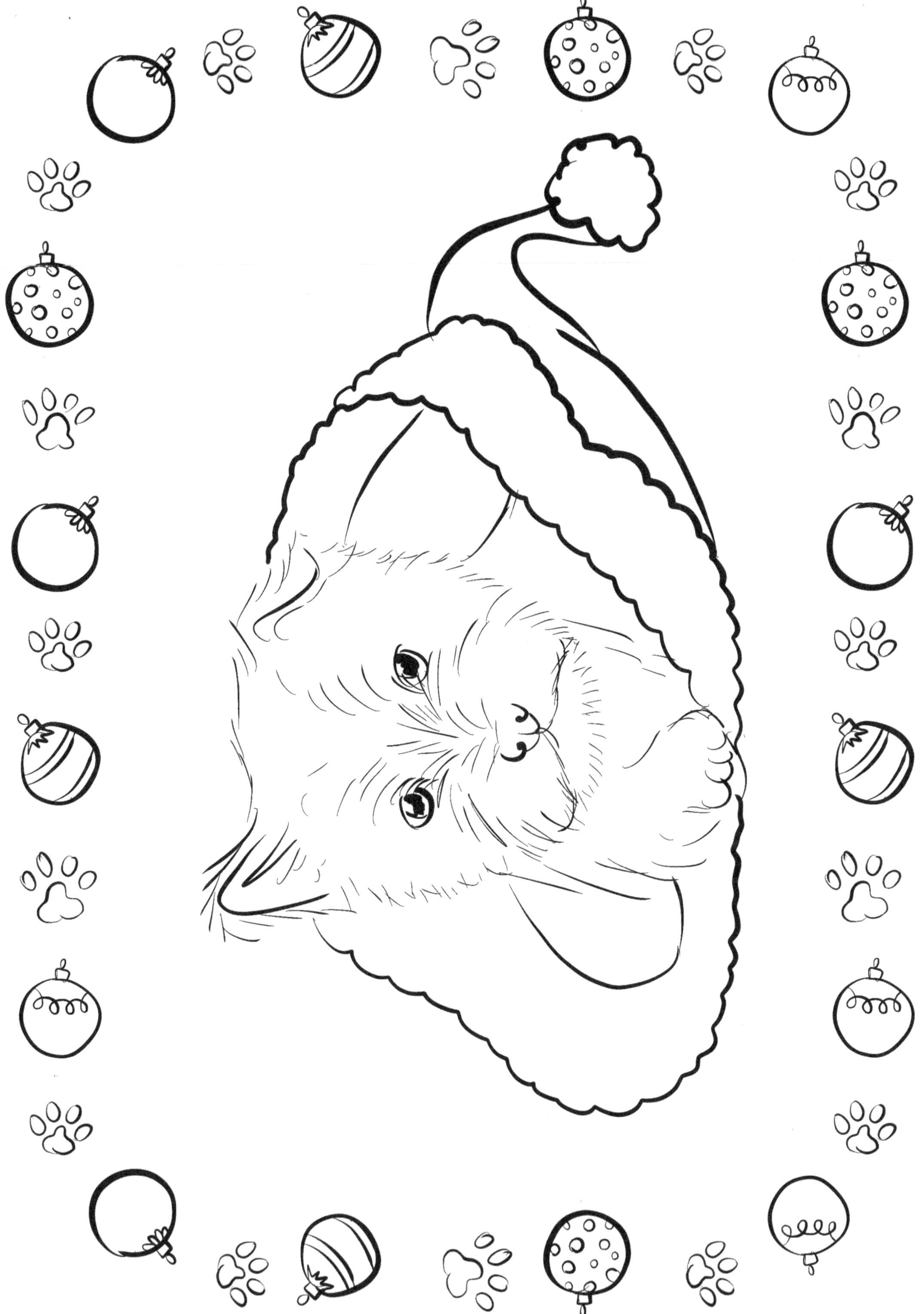

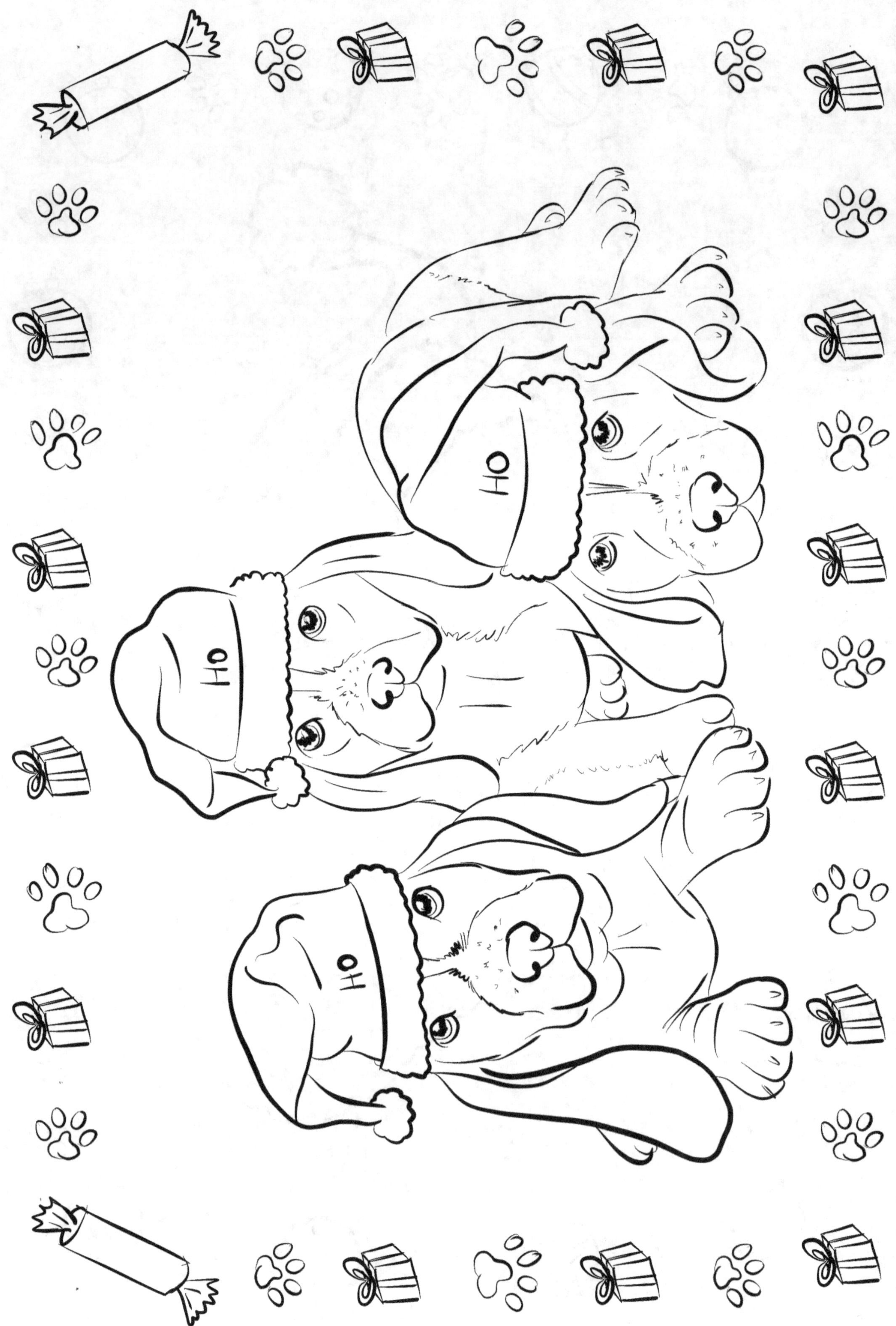

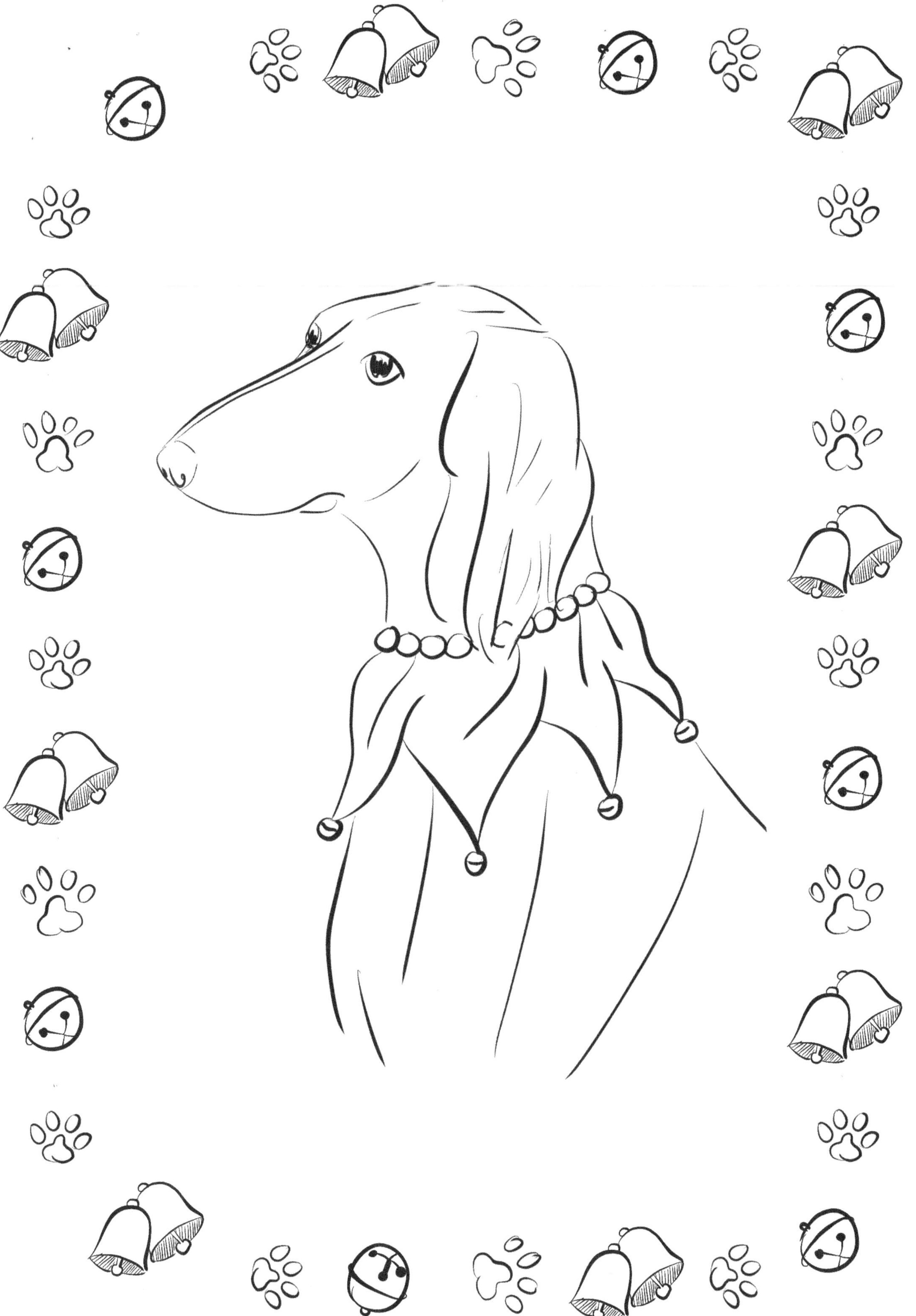

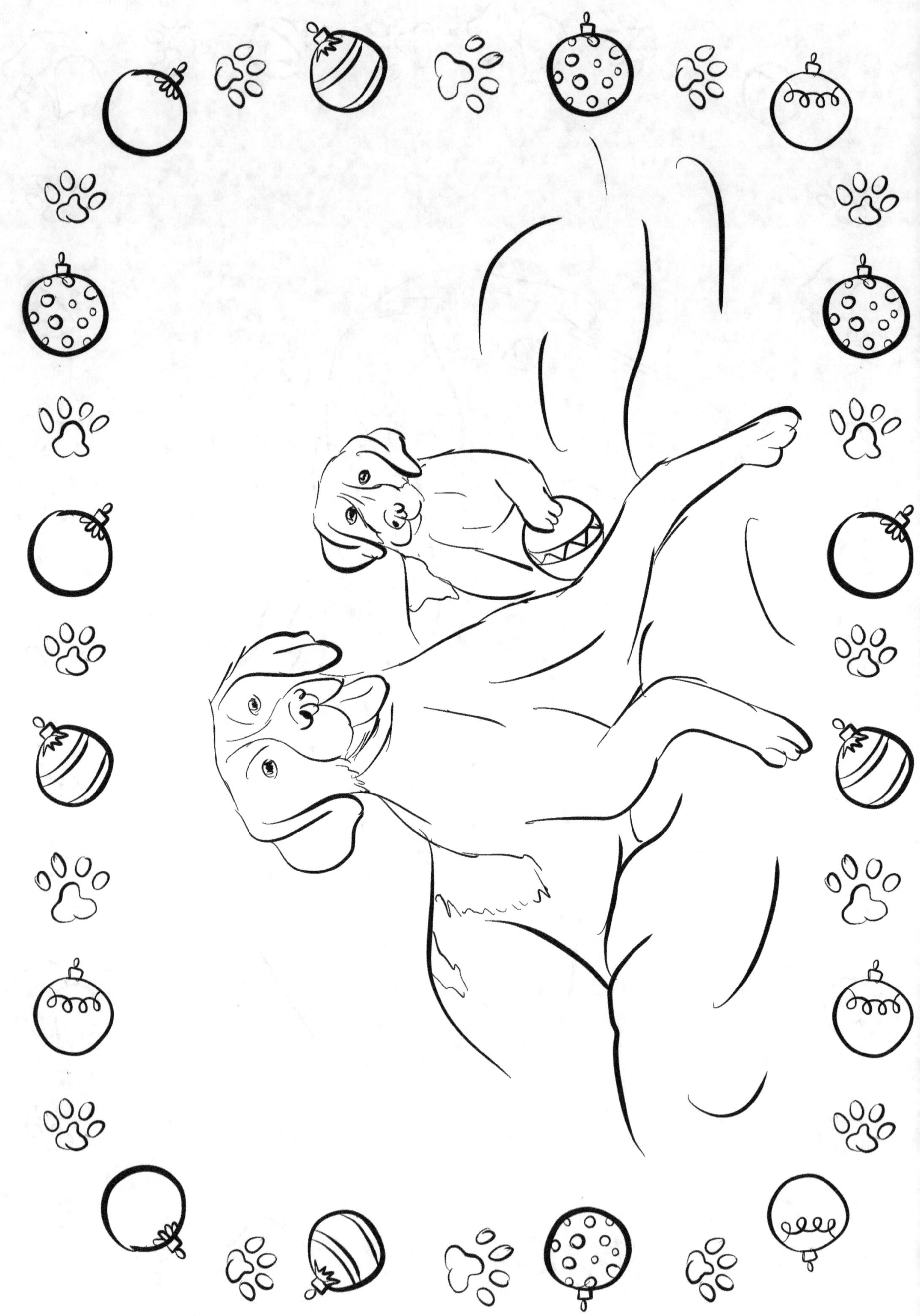

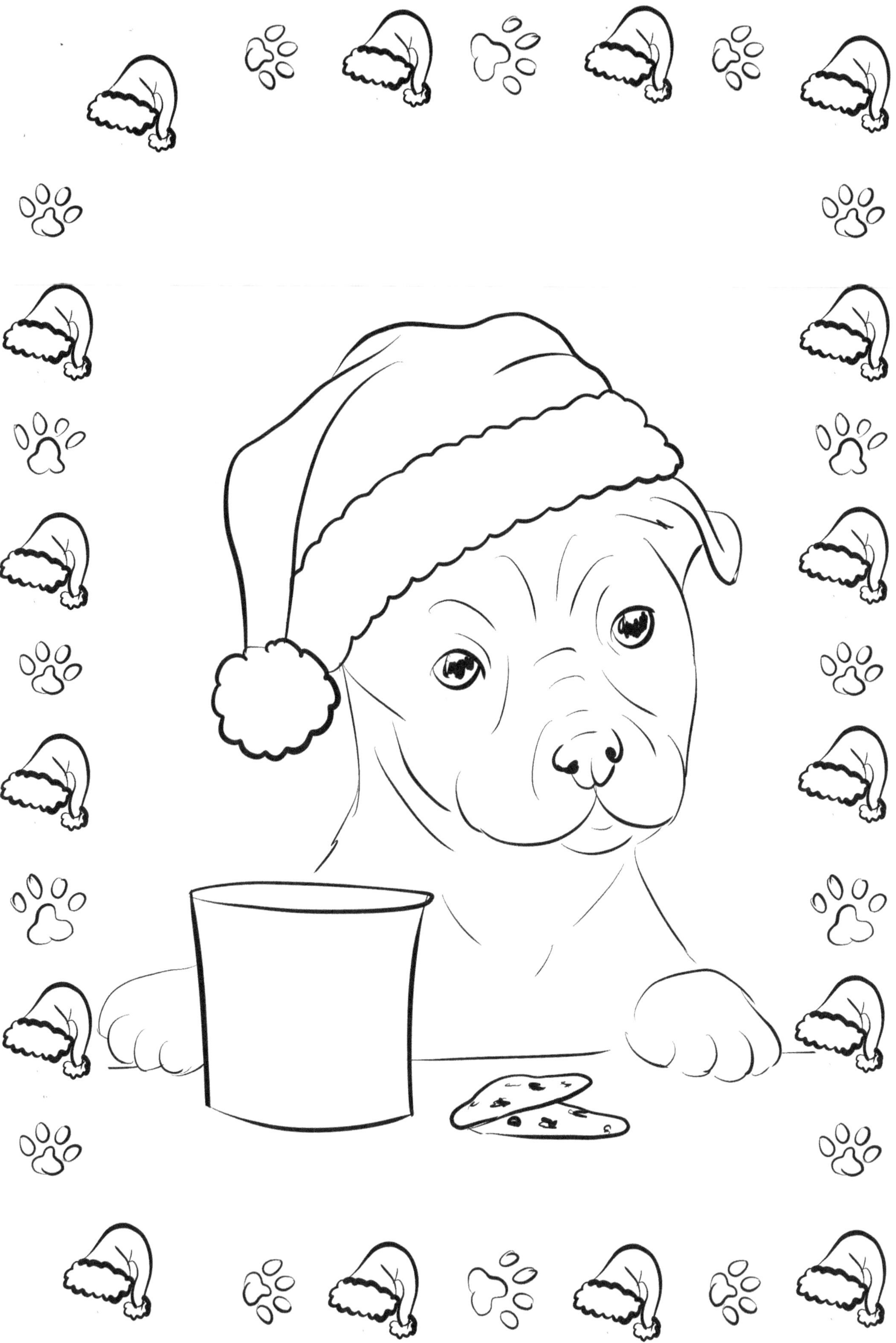

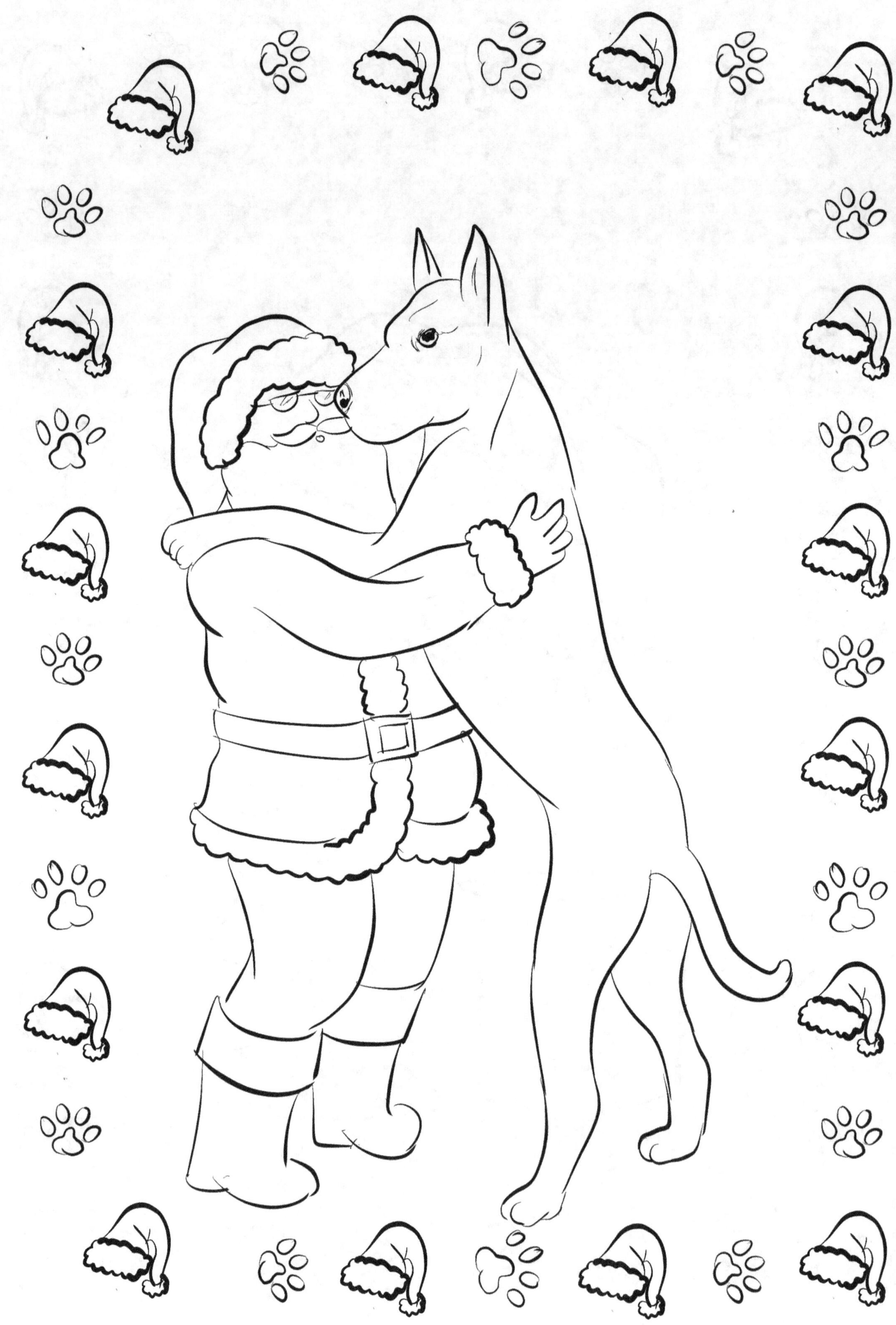

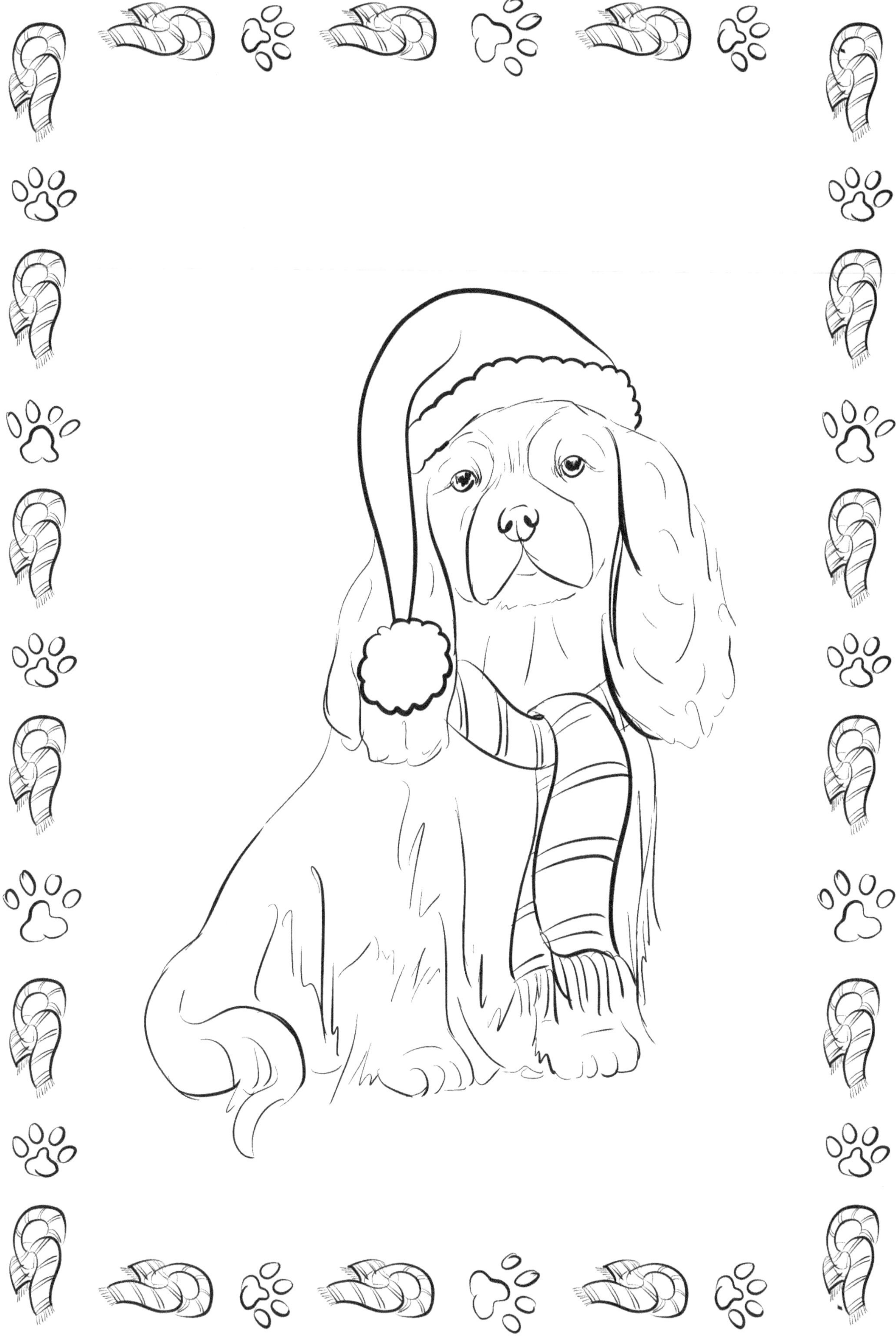

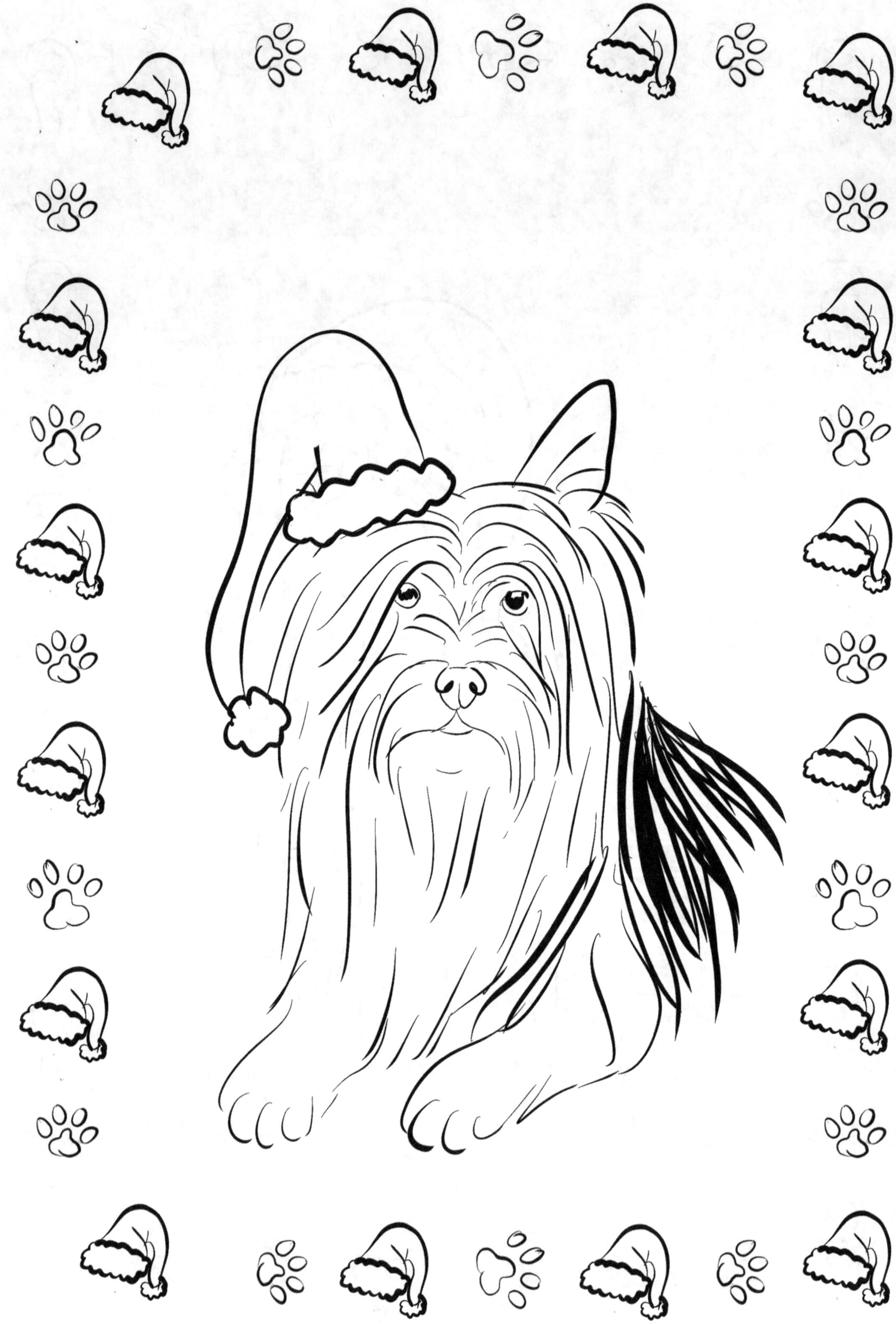

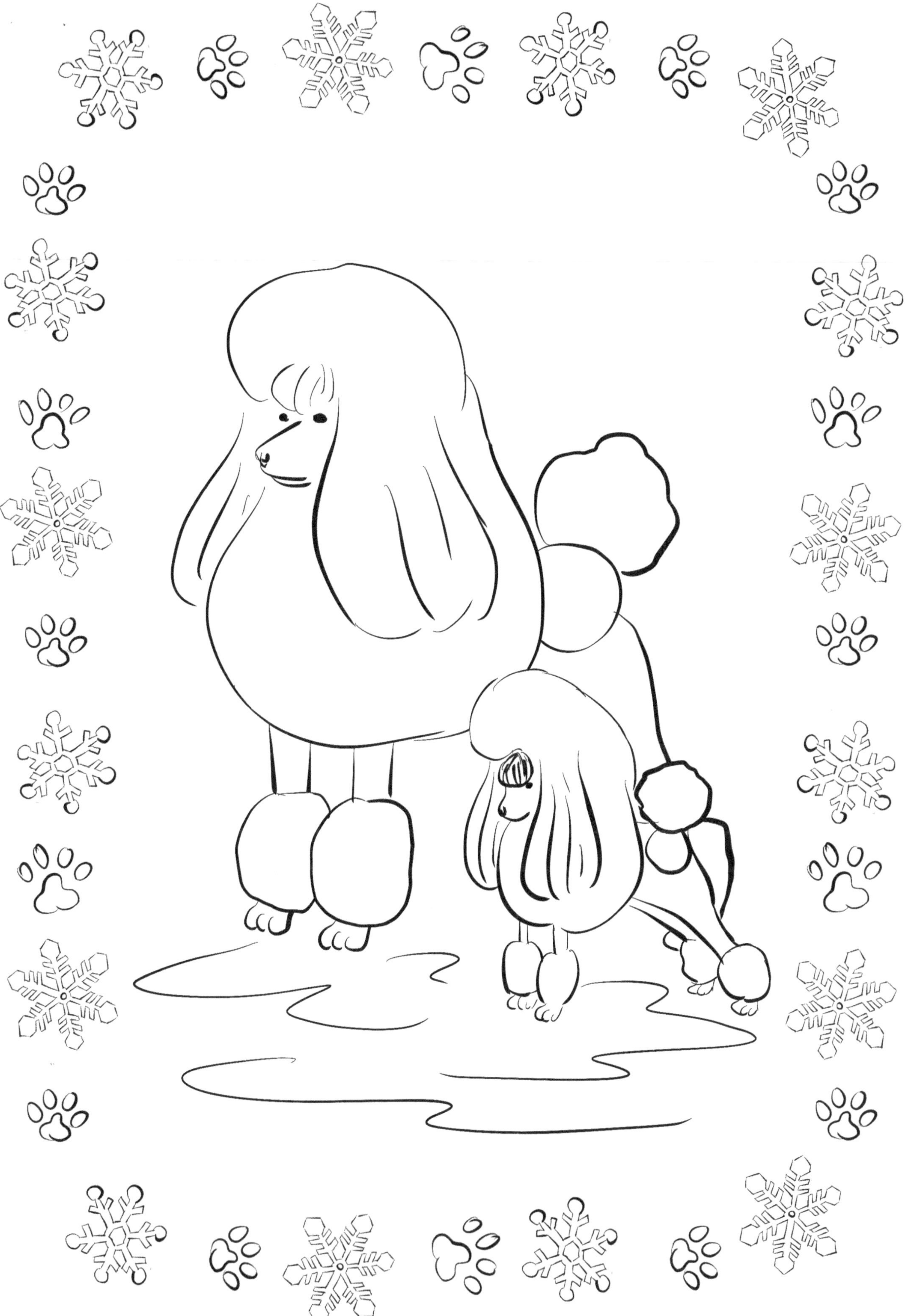

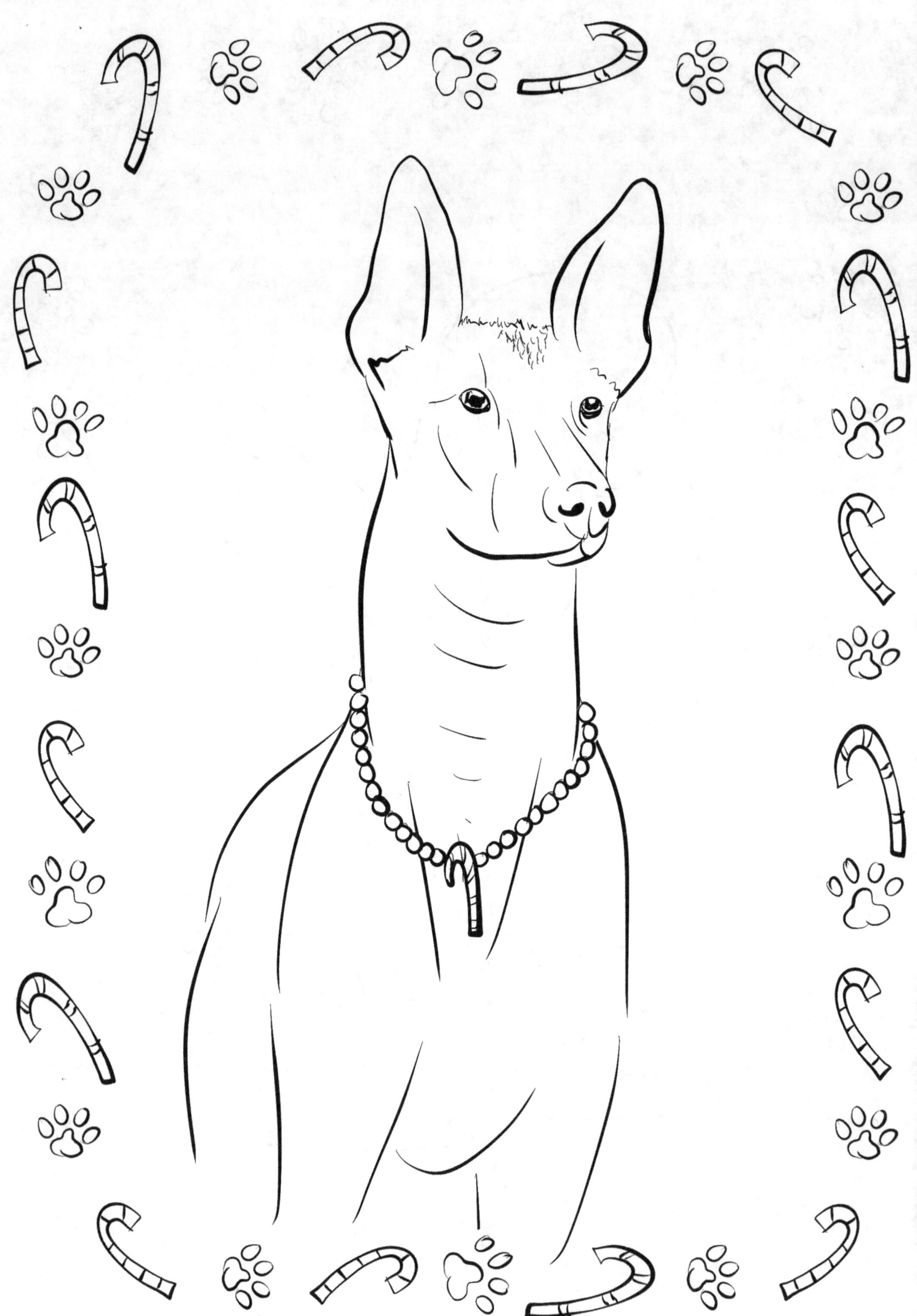

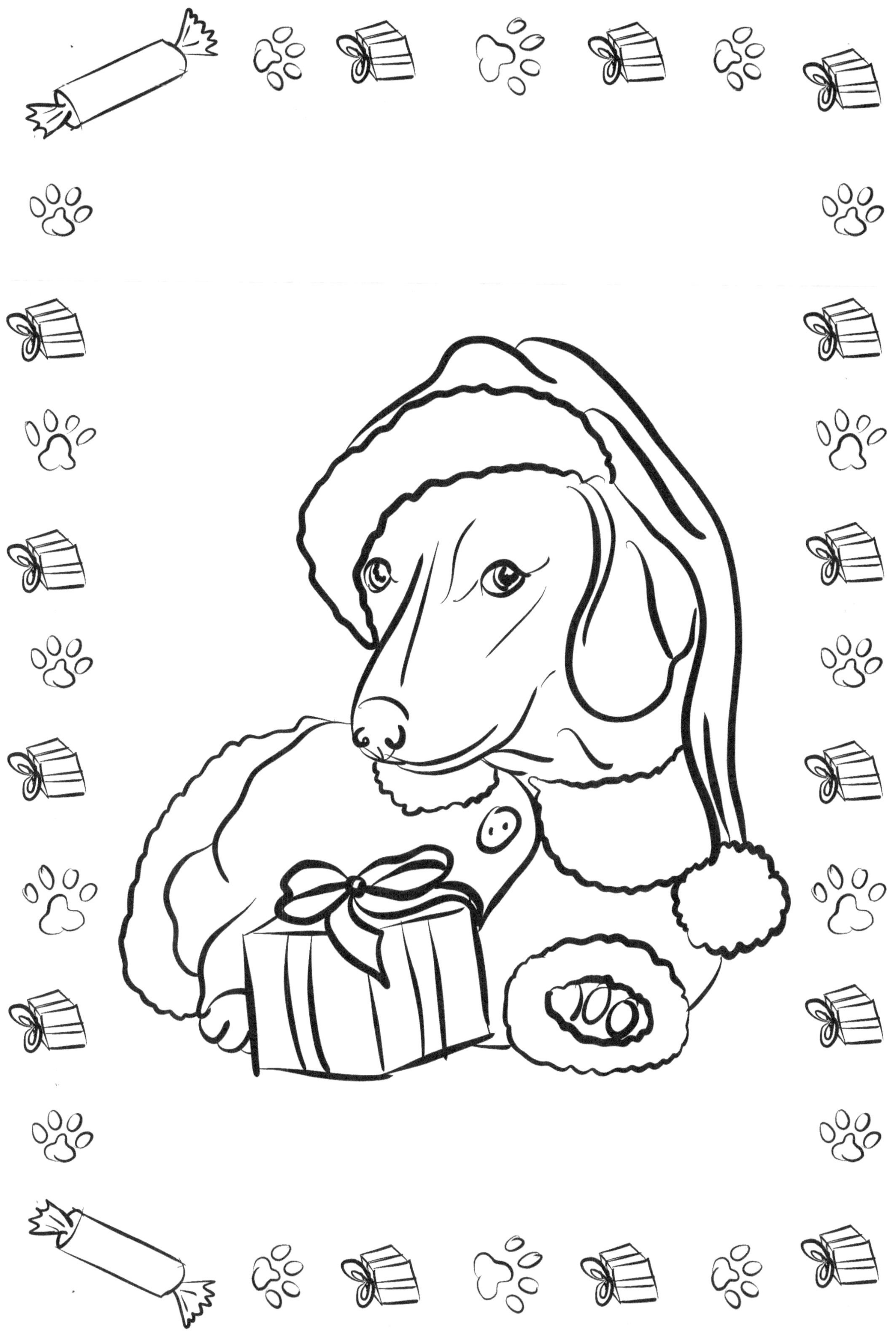

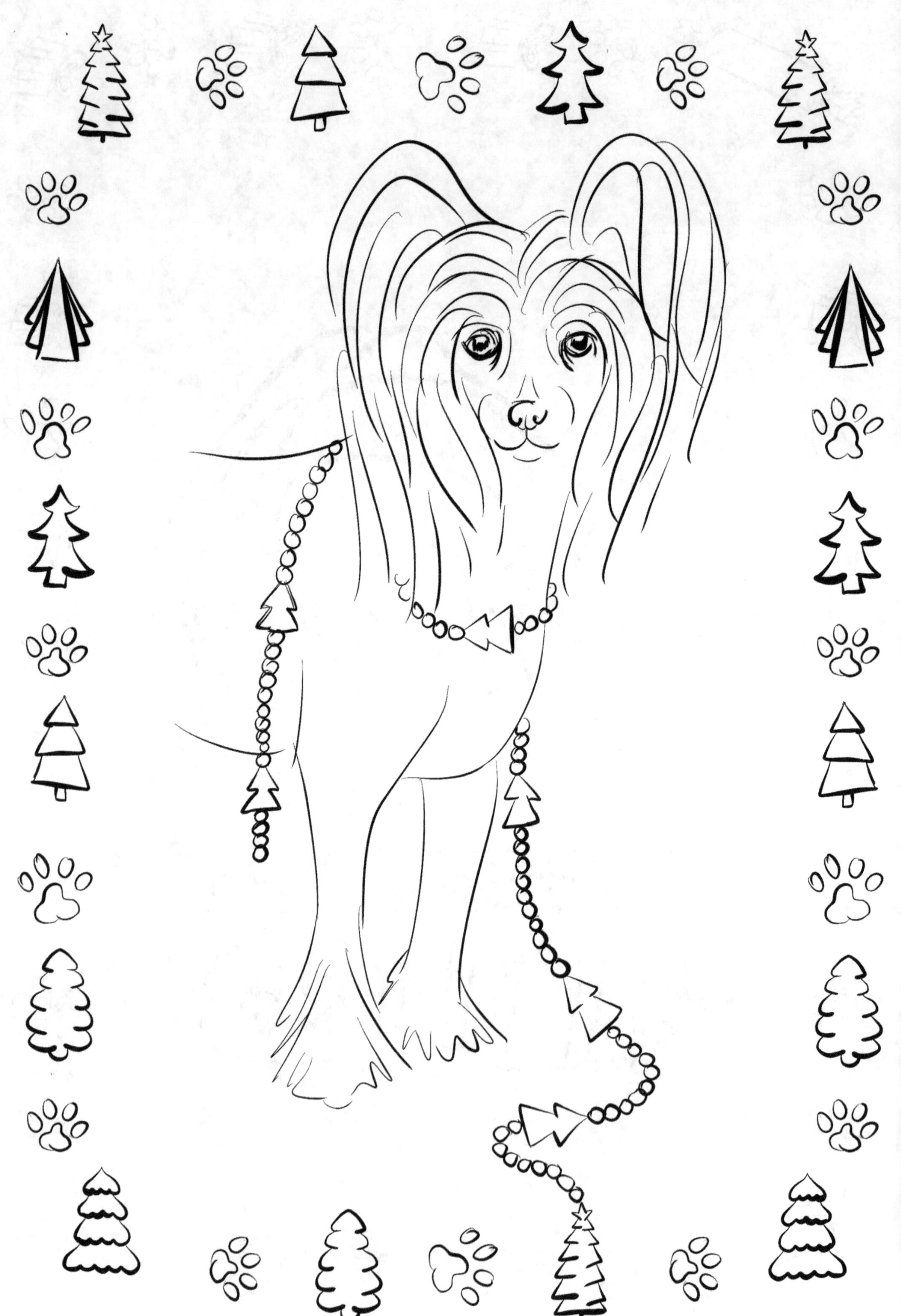

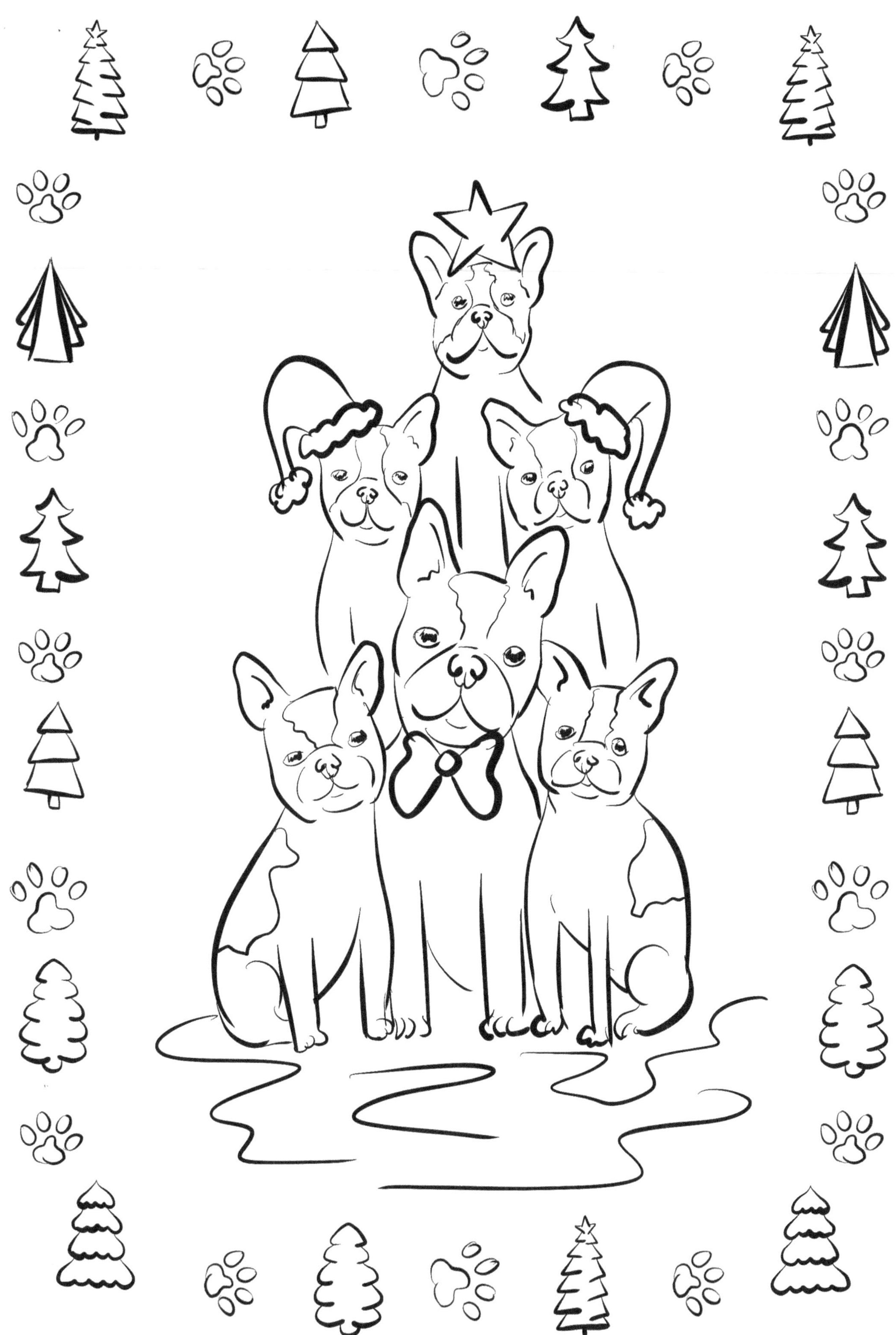

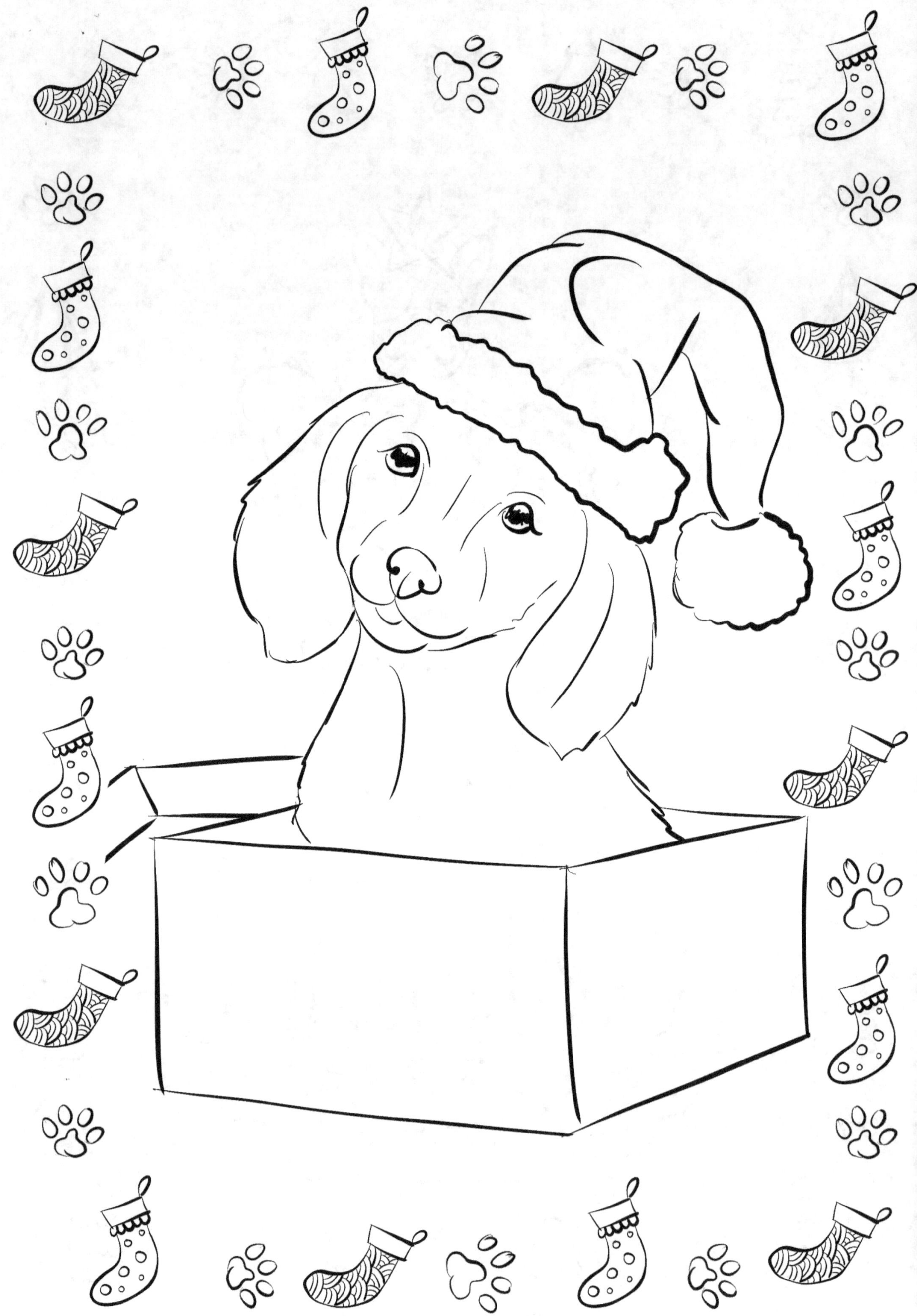

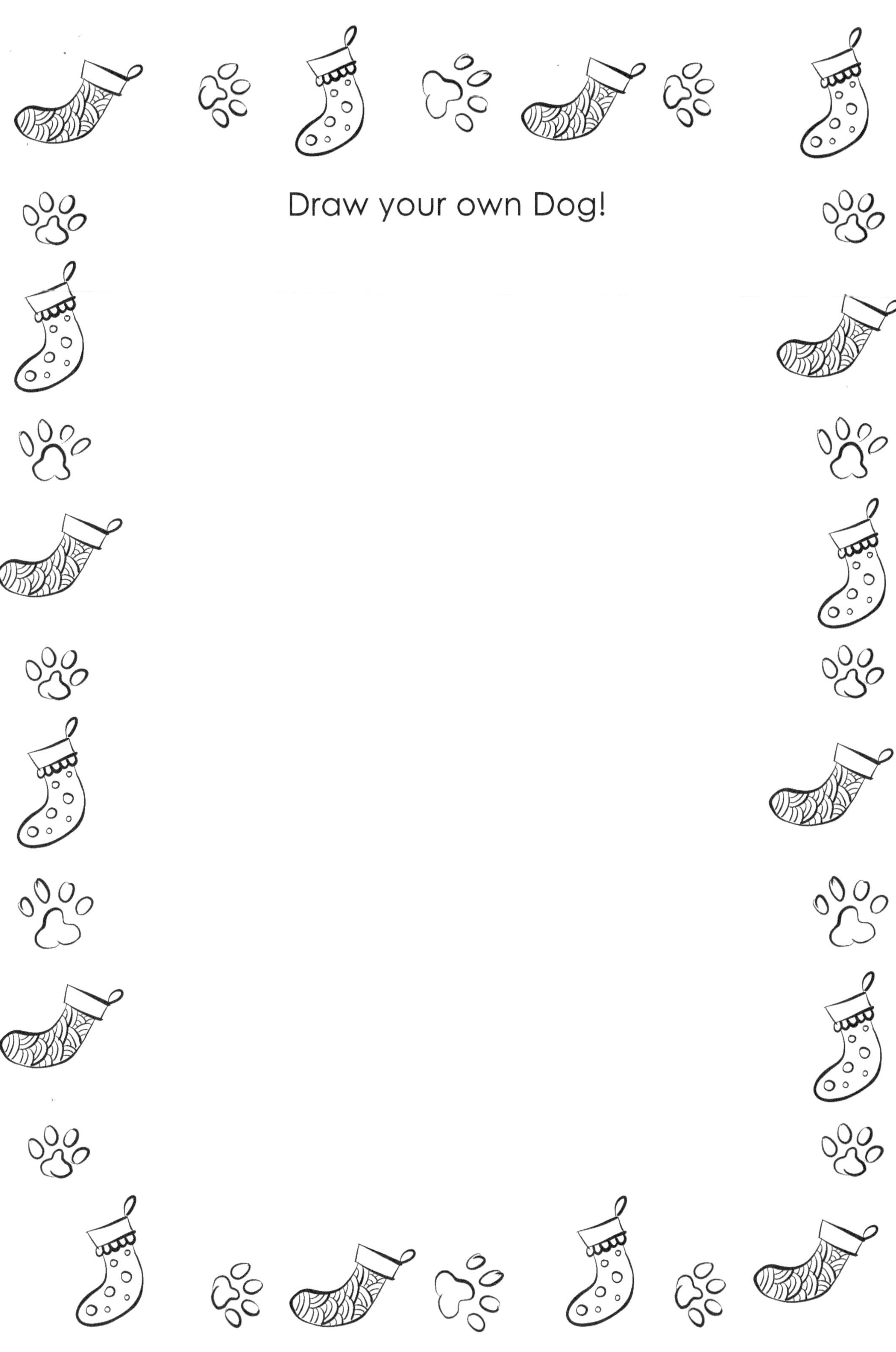

Draw your own Dog!

www.ingramcontent.com/pod-product-compliance
Lightning Source LLC
Chambersburg PA
CBHW080756030726

47593CB00007B/2397

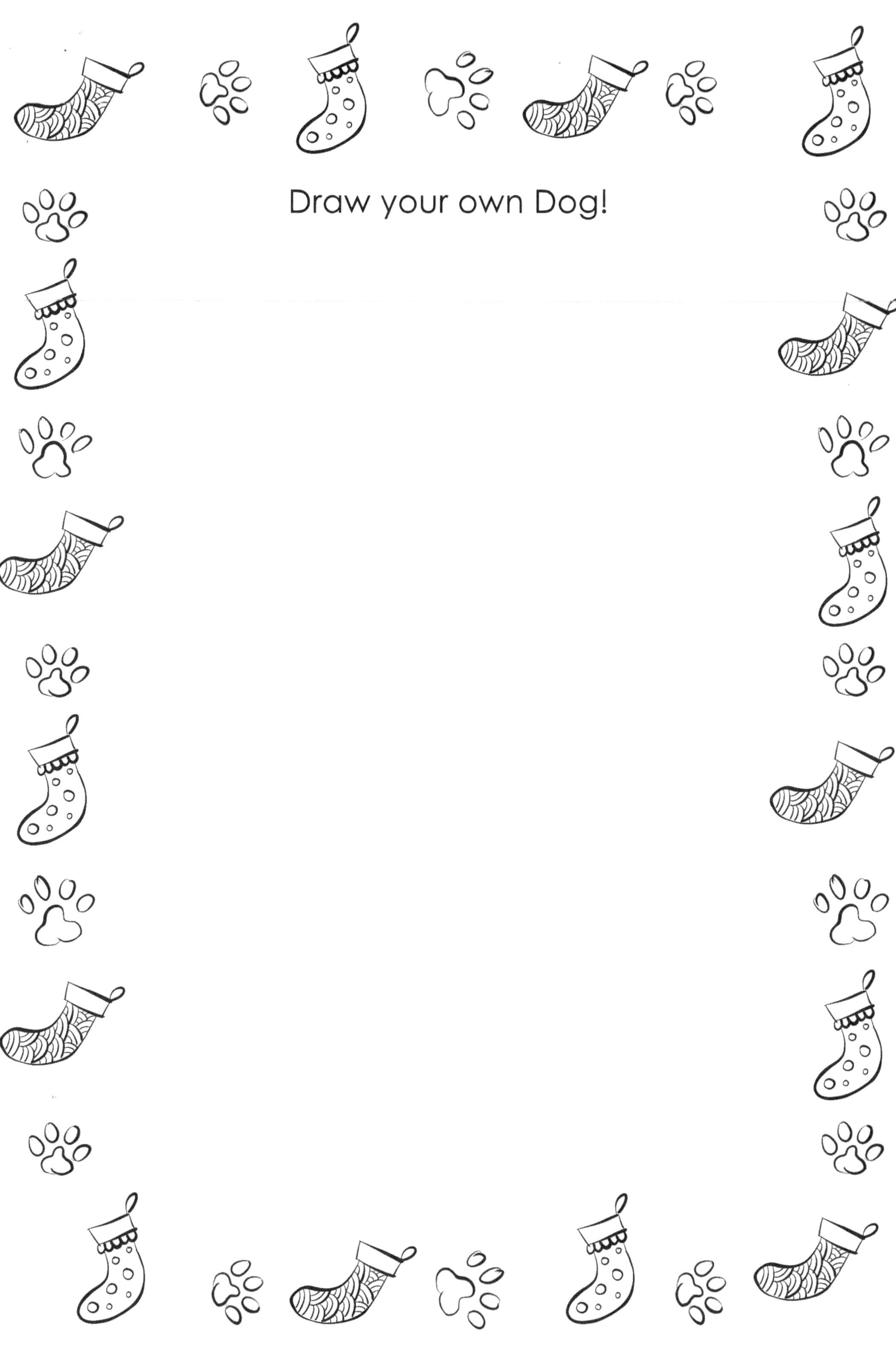

Draw your own Dog!

www.ingramcontent.com/pod-product-compliance
Lightning Source LLC
Chambersburg PA
CBHW080756030726

47593CB00007B/2397